FROM MY MOTHERS WOMB

BY UNCLE HECTOR

authorHOUSE®

AuthorHouse™
1663 Liberty Drive
Bloomington, IN 47403
www.authorhouse.com
Phone: 1-800-839-8640

First published by AuthorHouse 5/23/2011

ISBN: 978-1-4634-0803-9 (ebk)
ISBN: 978-1-4634-0804-6 (sc)

Library of Congress Control Number: 2011908752

Printed in the United States of America

TABLE OF CONTENTS

INTRODUCTION

This is a book of the true stories of my life I have used some of the real names of the people in this story. I have documented this story to the best of my recollection and exactly how all documented pages as they happened. Sometimes I have combined two or three stories into one. Perhaps one of the problems, you'll encounter when reading this book, I am talking about myself and about different subjects at the same time; nevertheless the stories are part of my life!

I began writing this book on September 13, 2009. I moved into an apartment to meditate seeking peace of mind. It was the only way to get away from the daily routine at home!

As the holidays approached that year 2009 I decided not to go home for Thanksgiving or Christmas! I preferred to stay in the apartment, meditating and writing this book. The decision was made almost automatically. My family was very upset and resentful, because I had leased the apartment for one year.

I have to admit that when the Holidays arrived, it brought tears to my eyes; family love is frequently reflexive and extremely conflicted. I believe that most people do not work on their love with their families; instead they accept it for what it is. In my case, it was the hand dealt to me that I had to play! I hope this book is an inspiration worth reading!

May the love of God Bless you always!

CHAPTER 1
ENGAGEMENT!

September 13, 2009, for the last four years I've been praying faithfully for the Lord to help me find a solution to my problems at home. Each day that passes by, it gets harder for me to control the situation of peace at home. So, I asked the Lord to show me and tell me what to do. God said through the Holy Spirit, you need to change yourself first before changing others! You are going into one year of exile. You need to continue your prayers and your meditation. I opened the Bible and the very first thing I see was what Paul said: "you are joined together with peace through the Holy Spirit, so make every effort to continue together in this way". It takes both God's power and our effort to produce a good loving Christian family. Unfortunately, I grew up in a family with unhealthy relationships. The Bible says, "Clothe your-selves with humility towards one another". Pride blocks grace in our lives. We must have God's grace in order to grow. Change, heal and help others. Paul advised live in harmony with each other. Don't try to act important, but enjoy the company of ordinary people, and don't think you know it all". Humility is not thinking less of your-self. It is thinking of your-self less. In church and every small group, there is always at least one difficult person, usually more than one. These people may have special emotional needs. God allowed these people in our midst for both to benefit. A family member different, but they are still a part of the group. In the same way the Bible says, "Be devoted to each other like a loving family. Excel in showing respect for each other; at this very moment, I am thinking about the word respect. In every family, there is a member of the family that for some reason or another is very disrespectful, not only with the family, but with everybody around them. My youngest daughter is a wonderful cook. She always invites the whole family for Thanksgiving dinner and on many occasions. The first ones to arrive at her house are my wife Geno and I. (Grand-ma & Grand-pa) and the last one to arrive is always my grand-daughter. She walks in like she is angry at the whole world. Everybody is doing something, like watching TV maybe a football or basketball game or playing with the dog. Within minutes she finds an excuse to begin an argument with her mother. Since the grand-parents are there, they get involved because of the disrespect against their daughter from the grand-daughter! Instead of getting the problem resolved, then the grand-parents end up arguing amongst themselves. This creates a problem, because then my wife and two daughters start bringing up the past, which is the biggest problem within the family no matter what the occasion is or the subject. I believe that life is all about learning how to love each other. God wants us to value relationships and make the effort to maintain harmony within the relationship. The Bible tells us that God has given us the ministry of restoring relationships. For many years I have been telling my wife that some day, I would like to write a book about my childhood and my experiences. My wife has been a very stubborn person. If I say something is black, she will say no it is white. That day she asked me, when are you going to write the book? I said I am waiting for the Lord to give me the sign. My oldest daughter was there visiting that day, she joined her mother in the attack! First my wife began by saying, make sure you write in the book the times you came home drunk and terrorized me and your children. Also all of the abuses you committed with us. I patiently said: As long as you keep living the past, you both will never be happy. As for me, I know who I was! I am at peace with God, and he forgave me a long time ago. You know you are maturing when you begin to see the hand of God in the random, baffling, and seemingly, painless circumstances of life. If you are facing trouble right now, don't ask, "Why Me" instead ask, "what do you want me to learn". Then trust in the Lord and keep on doing what's right. Happy is the man who doesn't give in when he is tempted but continues on the correct path.

I would like to begin!

When I was eighteen years old, my fiancée Genevieve Ramirez (Geno for short), wrote me a letter. She decided to move to New York, and wanted to terminate our relationship. I was so devastated that I went to the neighborhood store, where they sold wine, beer and rum. In 1948, the neighborhood store was the size of a two car garage. There were no entrances or doors, only a small window in the front. You had to order from the outside and pay first otherwise you didn't get served. I asked the store owner for a beer and pint of rum. He said where is the money? You know the rule is to pay first and be served. I said I have no money, charge it to my father; he is your best friend. My father was the loan shark. The way my father loaned money to the people, was very unfair. If you borrowed $10.00 dollars he would charge you twenty percent each week. He always told the borrower pay the interest first and keeps the principal and he was at that time my only role model. He always had two big illiterate bullies with him to collect the money. After drinking the rum and beer, I was intoxicated and violent. No one wanted to get near me. They called my older brother and father. My father came out of nowhere tackled me from behind, and threw me on the ground to restrain me. After my father and brother calmed me down I went home and tried to commit suicide by hanging myself. Luckily my sister Hilda was watching me as I put the noose around my neck prepared to kick the chair from under me, she let out a scream. My father and brother came running and stopped me.

I do not know if these events made my fiancée Geno change her mind about moving to New York City! But two years later we married. I began working at the Caribe Hilton Hotel in San Juan, Puerto Rico. I started as an air-conditioning installer, but within a month I became a foreman.

In retrospect, all of my life I have been an achiever. Achieving helped me to become a leader by accepting more responsibility. I was in the National Guard in Puerto Rico at the age of sixteen, attached to the 296th Medical Battalion, as a medic. I was then transferred to the 295th Combat Infantry Battalion, just after being married. I was transferred to the National Guard in San Juan Puerto Rico; I was living in Rio Piedras at the time. As soon as I got there I volunteered to be transferred to New York State National Guard. As soon as I got my discharge transfer letter, I went home and told Geno of my plans. At that time the governor of Puerto Rico was Luis Munoz Marin; who was married with President Franklin Delano Roosevelt's sister -in- law. The economical situation in Puerto Rico was very poor so the Governor of Puerto Rico was sending young Puerto Rican men to work the farms down south. One of them was my brother-in-law, Felix Ramirez, who was being treated as a slave, no food, water, and no beds to sleep were provided. They were eating raw vegetables picked from the fields! They called them second class Americans. After six months of labor from 5:00 am to 5:00 pm and minimum pay Felix finally decided to escape from the camps, we all decided New York was the destination for us. The problem was he only spoke Spanish. Together with his two friends they flew to the state of Ohio in a chartered plane by the Puerto Rican Common Wealth to work at the farms.

After, speaking with my wife, about going to New York City, I went to the airport to make the arrangements for the trip. At the time there were very few phones in the Island of Puerto Rico. The only way to communicate with other countries was by telegraph. As I remember I boarded the world war II DC 52 with about 20 passengers, one pilot and 1 flight attendant. The flight attendant was very short and poorly dressed.

The air plane took off early morning and went up in the air shaking and it looks like if it was going to fall apart. Four and a half hours later we landed in Miami. They ordered everybody out of the plane for refueling. We had to walk about 150 yards away from the plane for safety; they pumped the fuel from an old tank truck. A man climbed up to both wing of the plane where the storage tanks were for the gasoline. I remember that day very well because of one passenger that worked with me at the Hilton Hotel was on the flight. His name was Coldero (Red for short); it was not permitted to smoke inside the plane. We got out of the plane and right away he pulled out a cigarette and a lighter, put the cigarette to his lips, the flight attendant (as small as he was) jumped up and slapped him on the mouth and took the cigarette and lighter away! Red was too close to the fuel tank truck!

We left Miami only to arrive four hours later at La Guardia Airport, in New York. Upon arrival, my wife's cousin was waiting for me. They lived in the Bronx on Prospect Avenue. The area they lived was mostly an Italian neighborhood. The day after I arrived, I went to a candy factory around the Italian neighborhood. There was no application to be filled out. You just talked to the owner and tell him your age and where you were from. I explained I was from Puerto Rico and he said "another spick"! (I did not know the meaning of the word then). I was hired as a batch maker for the Candy Company. I worked six days a week eight hours a day. (Sundays Off), the pay was $32.50 paid every Saturday! Two weeks after I began working. I found out the meaning of the word spick, and confronted the owner of the word at the factory. I said to him I want you to know that my great-grandfathers' parents came from Italia and his name was Antonio Padrone. He then apologized and told me that I was a good worker and learned fast. I also told him that my grand-father was from the Canary Islands (Tenerife Lonerife) that was part of South Africa. My grand-father changed his name to Antonio Padron when the Canary Islands became part of Spain.

My wife had joined me in New York when she was two months pregnant. My wife started having labor pains; we walked down to the subway. We did not want to wait for the bus. We got to the hospital and they rushed my wife to the delivery room. She had our first baby. Hilda was born very healthy and beautiful on March 15, 1951. Three days passed by and my wife wanted me to take her home. She said that she did not like the hospital and the baby was not eating or nursing. I went to the office and told the nurse I was taking my wife and the baby home. The nurse said, No you are not! It is too early, I said yes I am! She agreed but had me fill out some paperwork that I was acknowledging that I was responsible once she was taken out of the hospital, so I signed the release papers and donated blood. I went to get my wife and the baby. I wrapped a blanket around the baby and went outside, to find out it was snowing very hard. We stood at the bus stop for about five minutes, before the bus took us to the apartment. When we went up and my aunt saw the baby, she fell in love with her and grabbed her very happily.

I continued working at the candy factory, when Hilda was eight months she began calling us by our first names. As she started growing and started kindergarten she began calling us mommy and daddy. She was 14 months old when we bought her a set of panties with the days of the week on them, Monday, Tuesday, etc. She knew the days of the week and wore them accordingly. She learned to wash them by hand and hang them in the bathroom. Before I would get home from work she would call her mommy and alert her that her daddy was coming home. Hilda was one smart kid!

To add to my income, I began working at a pharmaceutical company which meant a move from New York to Chicago, Illinois. The reason I ended up in Illinois, was because God had his plans prepared for me from the day I was born until the day he'll take me away. When I was born, my mother was a very sick woman. I was 18month old when she died at the age 32. I was also a very sick baby with malnutrition. My wife's aunt (Dona Carmen) was the mid wife that delivered all of my mother's seven children. She told my father that it would be a miracle if I lived and that my mother was not healthy enough to have any more children. My father brought home a woman before I was born to help my mom with the chores around the house and she lived with us. She took care of me like she was my own mother. My mother got pregnant again and the baby did not make it. I was told by my Aunt Carmen that before my mom died she begged her to take real good care of me, and not let me die! All the information I have and everything I know about my mother and my grand-father, I have to thank god for Tia Carmen and Abuelo Rafael. Aunt Carmen was the sister of Grandpa Rafael, father of my wife. When I was 10 years old I remember my Aunt Carmen asked me to have dinner with her family. Her husband was a Mason and his job was laying floor tiles. Those days the tiles were made of cement with color on top. I remember they were with four colors to choose from, green, brown, red and yellow. The majority of the people chose the green colored. Aunt Carmen's husband was tall and strong and did not like my father. They always argued because my father claimed that he built his home on my grandpa's land. One day they started a fight and my father was putting a good whopping on him until some of the workers from the factory came and stopped the fight. My father worked separate from them. I remember they called my father the PASTA MASTER. My father was having an affair with the maid before my mother died, and she knew it. As soon as my mother was buried, the maid started sharing the bed with my father and became his concubine! My oldest sister was eight years old and my brother was ten years old and I was 18 months when my mother passed I always thought that my step mother was my real mother, so I called her mom until I was 12 years old. My father came home one day and found this man, his last name was Mendez. He was hugging my step mother and they were in the dining room. This guy was very tall and very well dressed. He looked like an albino because he had very white skin, and was dressed in white clothes and shinny white shoes. My father hit this man on the face so hard, that he went thru the dining room opened window and landed on the ground completely out. Three guys from the factory came and picked him up and laid him on a flat bed truck and took him to the hospital.

The only two policemen in the area came. All they did was laugh and joke with my father. My father did not say a word to my step mother; instead he went to the neighborhood pub and got very drunk. When he came home he began beating my step mother. I grabbed his legs and started crying begging for him not to hit her. He threw me like a basketball against the wall. That's when he yelled at me and said. Why are you protecting her? She is not your mother! Your mother is dead because of you! He stopped hitting her, and left the house. My step mother came to me at that time; I was in a corner sitting a fetal position. She hugged me and told me the whole truth. I kept crying and talking at the same time. I kept repeating to "my step mother" "Why? I did not die at birth? Why? God, Didn't you let me die, and put me in the ground like a still-born child never seeing the light of day?"

My step mother kept stroking my head. She kept saying don't cry! You are going to live many years because God wants you to. My step mother was pregnant at the time, but I was so young and innocent that I never noticed. She gave birth to a boy that looked exactly like my father.

They named him Gonzalo Jr. But everybody called him Gony. That was the only child my stepmother ever had. He was also my father's favored son whom he played with him all the time. The abuse from my father to my stepmother and I continued. Several times she would pack a few things for us and go to her parent's big farm out in the center of the island. There the nights were cold. We dressed in sweaters and blankets that relatives and friends sent from New York. Since there was no electricity, water pipes, bathroom, no toilet paper; you had to wash your butt in the river, life on the farm was less than primitive. As always, my father would come to the farm three days after my stepmother and I ran away! He would take us back and where everything was normal until he got intoxicated again. It became a pattern. One day when I was 14 years old and my stepbrother was seven, my stepmother said to me. Tomorrow as soon as Gonzalo goes to work, we are going to get into the Pisicorre (public Van) and go to the airport. Somehow a friend of my father saw us walking with an old balsa wood suit case covered with cloth! He went to my father and told him my stepmother was already in the van and I started going in; I felt two hands pulling me back. As soon as the driver saw my father, he took off and I saw a passenger close the door of the van. I always believe that God was watching out for me. I never saw my step-mother again! Not long after the incident my brother began to laugh and taunt me; he would say "Ha! Ha! Ha"! You are an orphan for the second time! I was afraid to say anything because my father would probably have also killed me! After my stepmother disappeared; my father hired a lady to pick up the laundry and bring it back clean.

One day a young woman about in her late 20's arrived with my father to do the cleaning and cooking. The girl and her sister always came together to the laundry to pick up the clothes where I became more interested in the sister, now my wife, eventually Geno. I went to New York with my wife and my brother-in-law went to Chicago, Illinois. My brother-in-law Felix traveled along with our two other friends had saved over three hundred dollars, they were walking alongside the road and there was an older man standing by an old car with a for sale sign. It was a two door Plymouth. They paid the man 150.00 for the car. One of the two friends (the oldest) understood some English and using sign language; told the man that they did not know how to drive. So the man got in the car and showed them the gas pedal the brakes and the push buttons those cars had. They were forward, reverse and neutral. The man did not have a title for the car, no plates, and no information on the vehicle. They had no idea where they were or where they were going. Felix my brother-in-law is like my brother, we grew up together. We use to shine shoes for the rich people. Every penny that Felix would make, he would go home and give it to his mother.

His mother; my mother-in-law Angelina to be, was a very good Christian and was always praying for her family including me. She did not call me by my name. She always called me (Nene) like baby in English. God was the pilot of that car. After they received the instruction from the man that sold them the car they drove the car by the grace of God. They were parked facing north.

They were in a hurry to get out of the area so as the driver shifted to the letter "D" for drive they began heading North West. They only stopped four times to put gas in the tank at twenty-nine cents a gallon. When they got to Genesee Street in Waukegan, Illinois, right in the middle of a bridge the car motor exploded! A lot of steam coming up from the radiator, since they knew nothing about cars, they bailed out of the car very scared. Later they found out about that they did not check the radiator or the oil, so they drove until there was no oil or water left in the car!

After spending the night sitting by the car, which they pushed across the bridge, a man about in his early fifties came out of a big building, right on Genesee Street. He lived there with his wife and two teenagers a daughter and son. He was Mexican American and spoke Spanish. He told them he had the second floor of the building, and he had rooms for rent and also worked at the North Chicago hardware foundry. He suggested that they look there for a job, but we had to have some luck at that time. He actually took them in to look for a job. At the time the population in Waukegan was 58 thousand. Downtown Waukegan was like a cowboy town, and they had the electric street cars and no buses. Felix and his friends went downtown two blocks away. They went in to the restaurant looking for a job and the cook was a Mexican American. He talked to the owner of the restaurant and he hired them as kitchen helpers. They were paid fifty-cents an hour seven days a week, eight hours per day with no overtime paid. At the time they only paid ten dollars a week for the rented room and free food at the restaurant. Jack Benny the comedian was from Waukegan and ate at the restaurant frequently! When Jack Benny became famous, he moved to Beverly Hills Hollywood, California, and one day Felix was watching the thirteen-inch black and white television and saw Jack Benny, Felix said look I know that guy, he ate at the restaurant where I worked and told jokes all the time. After Felix worked one month and settled in at the restaurant in Waukegan and started to understand the language. He gave my mother-in-law his address in Waukegan. She sent the address to my wife Geno who wrote Felix a letter.

Two weeks later Felix wrote back and told me to go immediately that he was working at a hardware foundry and was earning $1.19 an hour. The work at the time by law was forty - eight hours a week with no overtime.

Hearing of that significant sum of money I bought my airplane ticket at Pan American Airlines the only airlines, flying to from LaGuardia Airport, New York, to Midway Airport in Chicago, Illinois. I took a taxi cab to Waukegan. I remember getting into Waukegan early in the morning a friend of Felix drove his old car to pick him up to go to work at the foundry they both worked. Felix introduced me to his friend and jumped in the two door car. Felix said to his friend, my brother-in-law speaks English, read and write. Let's drop him in front of the pharmaceutical company. I went in and I asked the receptionist for an application. She gave me the application and a pencil. I filled out the application quickly, gave it to her and she checked it out. Once in a while she would glance at me and smile. She said to me! Are you twenty one years old you are married and have a daughter? Yes I replied. She replied you look very young; do you have your birth certificate? Yes, I do. Then she said, okay, I believe you. She stood up and said I'll be right back. She took the application with her and returned in twenty minutes later with the production supervisor. He shook my hand and said, you are hired, would you like to start working today? You will be making $1.29 an hour, and forty-eight hours a week. I jumped up and opened my eyes in surprise and the manager asked what's wrong? There is nothing wrong I replied; it's just that I arrived from New York City this very morning and I have to find a place to stay! When Felix came home from work, I told him I had a job. To my surprise I found out I was the first and only Puerto Rican to be hired by that company!

The next morning I went to work, I arrived early at the company; they briefed me with the rules, and gave me a physical exam. They took me to the locker room, showed me my locker and gave me a uniform. It was mandatory to take a shower and wash your hair every day. My job description was chemical operator trainee for 90 days or three months. You had to qualify in three months in order to be a permanent employee. I wrote a letter to my wife because there were no telephones available to call her. My aunt was not very happy about taking the baby away from New York. She fell in love with the baby because she never had any children of her own. After getting my first check I sent the money to my wife, Felix loaned me fifty dollars so I could buy necessary things for the baby and wife. When my family arrived we began to learn about the area in which we would be living.

Three months passed, when my supervisor called me into his office. He shook my hand and said Congratulations! You are now a permanent employee and you are getting a ten cent per hour raise in your next pay check. (That was eighty cents a day and $4.80 a week). Steak at the time was nineteen cents a pound but I said to my wife, let's celebrate by eating! Another three month passed by and the supervisor called me to his office, shook my hand and said, I have never seen a person so clean and organized like you! I said to him, I learned this in the military. He began to laugh and said you are 21 years old, how long were you in the service? I replied five year. He laughed and said you know I don't like liars and I'm disappointed with you! I said, I will bring you prove tomorrow to show that I was in the Puerto Rican USA National Guard. I still had the transfer document from the Headquarters in San Juan, Puerto Rico to the Headquarters in New York State. Early next day I went to work with the letter and my honorable discharge and deposited in his box. About 10:00 am he came to me and said, when you finish what you are doing come to my office. What I was doing was horrible. I was alone in a room with four stainless steel wagons each of which was six hundred gallon capacity. The product I mixed was called anesthesin, and the main ingredient was benzyl and acetone. You hook up the steam hose to the jacket of the wagon and start the electric mixer. You heat it up to a certain temperature and turn the agitator off, remove the steam hose from the jacket and let it settle overnight.

It always left an odor on the "mixer". Upon completion I went to the supervisor's office and he greeted me with a big smile amazing!! He said! You were telling me the truth and I apologize! I want to tell you that you have been working now six month at the company and you never complained about what you are doing. You are the first person to last that long on that job! What you are working with is the main ingredient for anesthesia, used in the hospitals during operations. He told me; Hector we have three classifications for the operators, class A-B and C. You qualify and deserve to be chemical operator (B) with an increase of twenty cents per hour. I finished the week working on the four anesthesin in wagons! What a job it was, settling overnight it formed a crust half way down! What s strong smell, from the Benzyl and acetone vapors? With a long scraper I had to chop down to break the crust at the time, we had green rubber gloves and apron but no vapor mask. (OSHA did not exist then). There, I became allergic to acetone, with allergies lasting until this day.

I finished the week and was transferred to the reactors and condensator building. There, I was assigned to a chemical engineer to train me for two weeks. I worked with the chemical engineer for one year running his experiments with his written instructions. It was then the year 1952. I was transferred to a building called D-1 where they made the raw material for baby aspirin (still on the market today). I had been working very happy and everything was normal until one day in January 1953, my supervisor came to me and said someone is looking for you in the front lobby! I went and they grabbed me. Two FBI agents dress in black suits. One of them said to me, you are delinquent from the draft and the National Guard. I said how can that be? They never sent me a draft notice. He said they sent you a notice to your home address in Puerto Rico in 1950 to report to Camp Buchanan in Puerto Rico, you never notified the draft board of your address in the states.

I passed the test at the induction center in Chicago. I remember we were standing in line about thirty young men ranging from eighteen to twenty three years of age. I was the only one married with now two children and my wife was expecting our third child. One at the time in a single file, we stopped at the second lieutenants desk and he would call your name out. Ask very few questions. He would then stamp your papers; either rejected or accepted when my name was called, I stood in front of him in a military manner, saluted and he returned my salute. He told me that was not necessary. I said that is a habit from the military.

When I was standing in front of the officer at the induction center in Chicago, he said to me are you sure you want to do this. I said do I have a choice? He replied you have a choice because you are married with two children and a third on the way. I began thinking about my wife and how she was having problems with me going out drinking, fighting at the bars while she stayed home with the children. I said, maybe if I go away for a while things will change. I asked the officer, what choice do I have? You can get a deferment and you can join the

Army Reserves or you can go back to the National Guard of Illinois. I thought about it for a moment and told him I prefer to go with the rest of the guys. Ok! You are accepted and all of you will be going to Fort Sheridan for shots and processing. Fort Sheridan was a short distance from Waukegan where my family was living. But I could not see them for at least two years. My thought was if I get killed at least my wife, Geno would have my life insurance. We recruits boarded the bus in a single file with the Lieutenant calling our names as we entered the bus. We stayed in Fort Sheridan for one week and then we were taken by bus to Fort Lenard Wood, Missouri, for combat training. My wife Geno had to go back to Puerto Rico with the children because she could not live in Illinois with the Poor Army pay check.

After three months of training at Fort Leonard Wood. We were given a pass for two weeks and orders to report to camp Kilmer Port of Embarkation in New Jersey. I went to New York with another soldier that was new-yor-Rican (a name given to Puerto Ricans from New York) and we located my stepmother and three cousins.

I reported to Camp Kilmer on time and spent the next three weeks waiting for the ship to load up with supply and equipment for the Battalion. Finally, we boarded the ship and started moving. Everything was calm until we hit the middle of Atlantic Ocean. (I could not understand why they call that ocean the Atlantic. The waves were like big mountains coming at the ship). The ship went up and down and I thought we were going to sink. Everybody got very sick. I would be standing in front of the long mess hall table with my chow (food) tray, holding on to it because otherwise it would fly away. We finally docked in London, England to re-fuel we rested two days after a rough voyage and sailed again. My time came to go home. The company commander called me in his office and asked me if I wanted to re-enlist for another three years. I was getting a promotion and three thousand dollar bonus. That was a lot of money then. I am sitting in the apartment living room watching the five o'clock news. It is November 6th 2009 and they are showing the massacre committed by an army Major of Muslim descent when you are in the military; that does not mean that you are going to be killed in battle. Today with family television, newscasters, cameras, videos and modern technology, you can see the war right in your living room. Many things happened in the Second World War and Korea that people are not aware of. A big example of this is the Unknown Soldier. I remember that we were in Germany at the time firing range shooting the M -1, 30 calibers Garand Rifle. My squad and I were sitting in the bunker you have all combat equipment with you but no bullets. A young soldier sitting to my right, he looked pale and fragile. When we were ready to stand up and move to the firing range there was a (boom), I looked and there he was slumped with the back of his head splattered all over the wall. I never told my wife any of the bad things I saw or happened to me. All of the letters or mail were processed by the military and had to go thru censorship. One thing that I have not been able to get out of my mind is why? My wife did not answer any of my letters, when I was out there in the battle field at night and all you could see was the stars up in the sky. I would be laying down inside the pup-tent with my rifle and bayonet on my right side and the full pack on my left. You carry your mess kit, k-ration, cigarette lighter, a candle, first aid kit, writing paper and envelopes. I sometimes during the night while laying down, you could not sit or stand up. You would have to crawl in and out of the tent, and you had to sleep with your fatigues and combat boots on and your steel helmet was your pillow. During the winter you carry your sleeping bag it was called the roll and fart bag. Like I said before we would lay face down; grab our candle, lighter and an empty can of k-ration for safety. We carried two ball point pens inside our fatigue pockets. The next morning very early the First Sergeant would call formation and each platoon consist of eleven men, one squad leader. The platoon consisted of four squads and I was fourth squad leader. The company commander was in charge of four platoons, including company headquarters along with a total of one hundred twenty men. His rank was either First Lieutenant or Captain. I had an African American captain that played football in college. He was the one that asked me to join the all army boxing team. After we ate breakfast standing up outside with your rifle on your shoulder we had mail call. The Sergeant would call the names and you would answer here sir. Most of the time my name was not called and the guys on my squad noticed one day one of the guys said to me Hector you remember the picture we took together. I send them to my sister in Virginia. She asked me who the guy with you in the picture is. I told her that you were not only good looking, but that you are a boxer and also a good singer. Do you want to correspond with her? I told him you know that I have a wife and children, and I do not want your young sister to get all messed up with me. Two weeks passed and no letters from my wife, but I did get an anonymous letter from Puerto Rico telling me that my wife operated herself or closed down the "factory" after giving birth to our second daughter Abby. The letter said that her mother and the doctor begged her not to do it because we were young and very healthy. The doctor asked her if he could adopt the beautiful baby, because my wife did not want any more children. They were unattended or with a boy that was gay (pato) this letter became my next trauma. I planed then on making a military career in the Army.

I began drinking more than I wanted and got myself arrested by the military police twice. The army chaplain called me in and we prayed and talked. I told him about my problem. He asked me if I loved my children and wife. I told him that I loved my children and my wife. I went back to a normal military life until one day I was told by the first Lieutenant report to the S-2 intelligence section. I went in gave my military salute; to the two intelligence officer and two guards. They told me to sit down. The reason you are here is because we found your name and two of your friends stationed in Fort Hood, Texas on a list confiscated from the records of the meeting of the "Nationalist Group for the liberation of Puerto Rico", held in Chicago, Illinois. The same group tried to call attention by trying by force to get into the White House. They had guns and were shooting at everybody. Some of them were killed including a police officer.

I answered all of the questions. I told them that I haven't done anything wrong. I was restricted to my quarters until final investigations were completed. The FBI in Puerto Rico went to my wife's apartment several times but refused to tell my wife what was happening. They even talk to some of the neighbors in the town where I was born. They talked to my father and my brother a career soldier stationed at Camp Buchanan in Puerto Rico. Finally after three months of investigation they released me from restriction because they had no evidence for a court martial. After talking to the company commander and telling him that I wanted to go home to my family, he again said! You will have ninety days from the date of your discharge to come back to the military. I was shipped to Puerto Rico. When I arrived in Puerto Rico it was two weeks before Christmas. One day as I was walking to the mess hall, and I heard a voice of a First Sergeant telling the jeep driver, Stop, stop. That's my brother! A man got out of the jeep began hugging me. He took me to his house in the same camp. (The non commission officer and commanding officer had their military houses for the family on base). While at his house on base we talked about Christmas and New Years and caught up on the past years.

I told him that I was going to be discharged. On January 1st, 1955, I received my Honorable Discharge Papers. I was walking down the street with my Class A uniform and duffel bag on my shoulder. I saw this boy running in front of me yelling my wife's name. He was saying your husband is coming. I followed him to the building's second floor where my wife and children were living. I was very disappointed right away because my wife and children did not seem to be happy to see me. But I was the person that made that situation because I left without notice. The first night she was very cold and distant. The first morning was also challenging, my son was two years and eleven months old, when he saw me coming out of the bedroom, and he yelled at me a bad word in Spanish. I slapped his mouth and told him I was his father and he was not going to say that word again to me or anyone else. That was our first confrontation.

After a few minutes, Geno came out of the room; she told me that she owed some money to the owner of the grocery store a block from the house. She did not ask me, she just told me to go and pay him! I walked to the store and I asked the owner how much money does my wife Geno owe you? He immediately, replied don't worry about it you can pay me some other time. I said to him I guess you do not understand what I am saying. I want to pay you now! He said, I will get the note book, he told me the amount but it was over one hundred dollars which was a lot of money in those days.

I had been home for one week yet my wife was very strange to me. One day she told me that the woman that lived across in the other building was jealous of her because her husband gave her a ride in his car sometimes. Another day she told me that a man whistled at here every time she stepped out of the apartment. I told her that I was going to be watching and take care of "the whistler". As time passed, I did not see or hear anything, so I went to see my father; when he saw me he was not happy to see me. It was the first time he seen me in five years but there were no hugs, no handshake, nothing! All he said was "you are much bigger now!" I heard you were in trouble in the Army. The FBI came asking people about you and what kind of childhood you had.

I told my father, I hope you told them because you know my childhood better than anyone else. He looked down to the ground and I saw tears hit the ground. I turned around and went back to my wife and kids. That was the last time I saw my father for the next twenty years.

Three weeks later I went to see my oldest sister to tell her about my plans to go back to Illinois. Both of my sisters were school teachers. I talked to my sisters about our father and how he welcomed me. My sisters replied we know what the problem with our father is. He found out that our stepmother is living with a merchant marine in New York. I told my sister I know all about it. I visited them when I was in Camp Kilmer, New Jersey. This man when he saw me, he hugged me like if I was his own son. He said to me your mother (He did not say your stepmother) has told me how you survived after you were born. My sister then told me that's why my father was angry at me. I replied, my father, has been angry at me since I was born. Do you remember when I was twelve years old they rushed me to the hospital, I got food poisoning. My stepmother was crying, and my father was standing there like nothing was happening; when they took me to the hospital I was in convulsions and trembling. They rushed me into the emergency room. They pumped my stomach and gave me a bath in a porcelain tub. I said to my sister to this day I believe my father put rat poison in my food, after that happened I did not eat at home anymore. My wife's aunt (the midwife) gave me food. Sometimes with a sling shot made from an inner tube of a bicycle in those days at the farm there was plenty to eat such as birds, rabbits, chickens, eggs, guinea pigs and plenty of fruits. I put three rocks on the ground and cooked the game I killed with my sling shot. There was plenty of fish by the river where I went swimming. Sometimes I would take an empty can of Quaker oats; they were three times as big as they are now. I would start the fire with dry pieces of tree branches placed in the center of the three rocks. I take a large piece of glass from a bottle; face the glass to the hot Puerto Rican sun. I always put pieces of paper on top of the wood. In a matter of minutes the fire got started and I proceeded to put pieces of homemade charcoal on top of the fire. I cooked fish soup with onion and carats, rice, potatoes, cabbage. I learned of this with the boy's scouts, when we were at the jamboree camp.

Yesterday November 13, 2009 I cooked the fish soup with the same ingredients but in a different environment. I am now in a nice apartment, with a stove, refrigerator and plenty of dishes. After visiting my sister and telling her that I was going back to Illinois; she said, Hector, why don't you go back to school, under the GI Bill and finish your school? You are the only one in the family without a college degree. I told her, I do not want to stay in Puerto Rico, too many bad memories of my childhood. I can make a good living for my family and myself in Illinois. My wife's family, are in Illinois. They know me since I was twelve years old. They are a Christian family, very humble and they are going to give us shelter until I find a house to rent or buy. I remember when I was 14 years old. My mother-in-law was member of the Pentecostal church. At six o'clock, on Saturdays evenings, they would come and worship right under the street light. My father did not like them at all. Every Saturday my father would prepare buckets of water to throw at them. I sometimes joined them and sang with them and clapped my hands along with the congregation. I really enjoyed the music, and every Saturday I was waiting for them to arrive. One Saturday my father threw three bucket of water at them, and could not stand it any longer. I yelled at my father, these people are not bothering anyone! They don't even say anything to you when you throw the water at them. They just keep on singing, leave them alone. My father had a few drinks in him and he came after me, I tackled him by his legs and knocked him down. I took off running and for the next three months, I slept in cardboard boxes and sometimes on top of the tall stack of flour sacks in the warehouse where my father worked. My father was the master baker and part owner of the factory. They worked three shifts and manufactured bread and pasta for Puerto Rico and the Caribbean islands. My father could care less where I was. One night a worker was coming into work for the late shift. He saw me going into the warehouse he followed me and saw the baseball bat I was carrying. He went and told my father, and my father came. He said, I know you are up there, come down! I said I'll come down if you promise that you are not going to beat me up especially to my Uncle Fernando. Uncle Fernando was my step-mothers uncle. He lived nearby in one of the houses my grandpa left when he passed. Uncle Fernando hated my father, and they were always arguing because he did not like the way he treated my stepmother and me. My stepmother and I went one day to Uncle Fernando's house to hide. My father came looking for us and uncle went after my father with a butcher knife. After my father left, I came down from the stack of flour. I went home to my small bedroom and pushed the army cot against the closed door. I lay down with the baseball bat near me because I did not trust my father! Up to this very day I still have that trauma! Every night before I go to bed I lock the door with a chair or a broom stick and then place a loaded rifle near me with a nine bullet magazine and one in the chamber. I tell my oldest grandson that I always sleep with one eye open. I went back to school the next day because I wanted to see my dream girl, now my wife! I was in the eighth grade and had better than average grades. My best subjects were General Sciences, English and mathematics. My worse subject was Spanish, because I did not like to read the novels and then write a resume of what I read. One day the teacher asked the class if any of the boys wanted to volunteer for the home economics class. I raised my hand and that was a big mistake. I thought that my dream girl was going to be in the class, but she wasn't. The class was for a period of three months. You learn how to cook, how to make an apron and how to repair furniture's. We were outside one day, nine girls and I was the only boy. I had my apron on and we were working on our last project to complete the course. I was scraping a mahogany dining room chair and sanding it, to varnish it. All of a sudden a group of boys and girls including my dream girl were laughing and making fun of me. One boy that I knew was interested in my girl, called me a sissy. I removed the apron from my waist, threw it away and before I got to that kid my teacher grabbed me. I left and never finished the project. To my surprise at the end of the year they gave me a "B" plus for the subject. I went the next morning earlier than usual to school and hid behind the hibiscus bushes when the boy that called me a sissy came with his friend. I jumped on the boy and his friend; they took off running to tell one of the teachers. Two teachers restrained me and took me to the principal's office. I was suspended for one week. I did not want to stay around my father, so I went to my grand-parents farm out in the Island. My grandfather told me, to not be stupid and fight during school hours, instead catch the boy after school, away from the school grounds. I did not like other boys staring at my dream girl! At the age of sixteen I began walking with her to school. She had to pass in front of my house on the way to school. When my dream girl turned twenty years of age she became engaged to an army sergeant military police. He was ten years older than her, and twelve years older than me. He gave her the engagement ring, he bought her the wedding gown, and he had a complete furnished house. He had everything, but not my dream girl! Two weeks before the wedding she returned the ring and wedding gown.

When my wife gave birth to our third child, his wife was at the hospital. My wife told me later that his wife was his second cousin. When I came back from overseas in 1955, he was waiting at the same camp Buchanan to be sent overseas again. He saw me and came to me and asked are you, Hector, you look taller and also much bigger! He joined the Army in 1940 and my oldest brother went in 1941. My brother was drafted while attending the University of Puerto Rico. The year 1941 was when the Japanese attacked Pearl Harbor destroying all of the USA Ships and airplanes at Pearl Harbor. The President of the United States at the time was Franklin D. Roosevelt. He declared war against Japan and Germany. The United States was not prepared for a World War! The president immediately ordered all men from eighteen to fifty to be drafted into the armed forces. He ordered all of the automobile Industries to stop making cars. They started building war planes, destroyers, ships and all kinds of armament. The United States Patton tank was no match for the German tank. I remember the infantry shooting the 50 caliber machine gun trying to disable the tracks of the tanks.

When all the men went off to war the women had to take over all of the jobs at the factories. There were no cars made from nineteen forty two to nineteen forty five. In (There have been many written accounts of this time frame after the Pearl Harbor attack by the Japanese). In 1945, the President, Harry S. Truman dropped two atomic bombs, one of Hiroshima and Nagasaki, Japan. With the devastation of the atom bombs, the war was ended.

In 1950, five years after the Second World War ended, the USA was involved in the war with North Korea. After Korea came Vietnam.

My oldest brother Ralph participated in all three wars. He also participated in the Bay of Pigs invasion in Cuba. He was in charge of the communications center during the conflict, was about 300 yards off the beach head, where the exiled Cuban invaders along with Puerto Rican volunteers were going to begin the conflict "As explained by my brother". The U. S. Air force based in Orlando Florida was ready to take off to support the troops by air. President John F. Kennedy was supposed to give the signal for the air force to take off in support of the invasion. The signal for the support aircraft to take off never came! My brother with tears in his eyes was telling me that Castro's Army had deep trenches alongside the beach and the Area was off limits to civilians and guarded twenty-four seven. When the troop landing force was approaching in their boats, Castro's troops were waiting for them; they open fire killing everyone in sight. My brother said he was in shock, not moving! He was dressed with Castro's Army fatigues and had a heavy beard and a .45 pistol on his waist. He had a jeep camouflaged. He got in the jeep and drove back to Guantanamo bay. The guards also had the daily pass word to use, upon return to the Guantanamo Bay for access to the base. After I was discharged from the Army in 1955, I did not see my brother for the next twenty nine years. My step brother and my oldest brother were together most of the time. After attending the University of Puerto Rico for one year, he decided to join the Army. Both brothers were at the same camp and they were boxing for the same team. My stepbrother stayed in the Army for six years. Two of the six years were in Germany. His oldest son was born in Germany. Twenty two years later the Son completed his bachelor's degree at the University of Puerto Rico. He joined the Army and got married. The history is repeated again. His first son was born in Germany, now my step-brother had a son and grandson born in Germany. After my stepbrother spent twelve years in the military he decided to get out and join the police force in San Juan Puerto Rico. He became an expert with the .38 caliber revolver and took the silver medal at the Pan-American games. While patrolling his area in San Juan, for all kinds of crimes, he encountered a problem with a criminal that everyone feared, yelled profanity at my brother while he was on duty. My brother approached him, and asked, what is your problem? The criminal said that he was his problem, and immediately pulled out a butcher knife. My brother ran to the patrol car, but the guy kept coming. My brother said to him, stop or I will protect myself. My brother shot the criminal in the belly. My brother was a police sergeant at the time. After the incident he started having mental problems and was placed in mental institution. I flew from Chicago to San Juan, Puerto Rico to visit him. I went to see him in the institution he was being treated! When I saw him in the condition he was, and in a straight jacket, I began to cry. It was exactly like a jail cell. He was all alone in the ten by twelve room; next to him was a man that constantly yelled profanity. My brother recognized me and motion with his index finger to come to his cell. I got closer to his cell, he whispered in my ear! Hector; be careful not to go near that guy. He has tuberculosis and he is possessed by demons. When people come near him, he spits blood on them. When the guards come to tend him, they have to wear a plastic suit and a face shield. Then he said to me, I know you've had a rough childhood and you are an orphan two times. I said to him that's not true, our mother is living in the Bronx, New York, and she married a merchant Mariner younger than her. I met him in New York and he treated me like his own son. Then he said, I know all about it, our father told me that he wrote his testament and you are not included. I told my brother, you and everyone else know that my father hated me from the day I was born. You are not telling me anything new. Yesterday I went to see the house where you and I were born. It was a horrible moment for me; I tried not to cry because it brought me very sad memories. At the same time I was very happy because I was standing at the same corner where I waited every morning for my dream girl, and walked to school with her. I talked to some of the bakers and pasta makers that worked at the factory across from the house. My father was already retired from the company. He had the house where I was born rented and three houses in a very big lot, all the houses were rented. Two of the houses were rented by the bakers that I was speaking with one of them. They said to me Hector, we are not supposed to tell you of what we are about to let you know your father wrote a testament and we are the two witness. We talked to him and even begged him not to exclude you. All he said was that you are a traitor and the reason why he lost his two wife's. I asked him why you signed. You, know your fathers character he threatened us and said if you do not sign, I will kick you out of the houses. I told them that it was no surprise to me and my wife and I were doing very good, we had three children. They told me that they saw my children in Puerto Rico and I had a beautiful family. I have been blessed from the womb of my mother until this day. Today is November 19, 2009 in seven days some people will be celebrating Thanksgiving Day. For the last ten years we have celebrated Thanksgiving with my youngest daughter, my oldest daughter and I talked about this event and we both agreed not to attend the dinner because Thanksgiving should be celebrated every day. Every morning before I get out of the bed I wake up always between two or five in the morning. I lay in bed for the next two hours with my eyes closed. I begin meditating and it feels like if my spirit (Soul) comes out of my body, then I see it go up and up. It disappears and it feels that I am asleep but I am wide awake. I open the Bible and the lord directs me to the book of Ecclesiastes chapter 2-12, to 16: Then I turn my thoughts to consider wisdom, and also madness and folly. What more can the Lord does than has already been done? I saw that wisdom is better than folly, just a light is better than darkness. The wise man has eyes in his head and walks in the light. While the fool walks in darkness. But I came to realize, that the same fate overtakes them both. Then I thought in my heart, the fate of the fool will overtake me also. What then? I do again for being wise! I said in my heart, this too is meaningless. For the wise man, like the fool, will not be remembered, in days to come, both will be forgotten. Like the fool, the wise man too must die! After my stepbrother told me about my father calling me a traitor! He said to me, I want to tell you something. Promise me that you will not tell anyone. I agreed there is nothing wrong with me. I am just faking and acting crazy to get a pension from the government. After six months at the institution. He was put on valium and other medications. He received his pension and his wife went to work. His father gave him the money to buy land out in the country. He built a beautiful house way up in the hills, overlooking the express way. He dedicated himself to raising roosters to fight in the arena where everybody bets a lot of money. My brother once told me that the cock fights were a gentlemen's sport. I went to visit him one day and he was butchering a large pig about two hundred pounds. I asked him what you are going to do with all that meat. He said, all that meat is sold already. He told me that he did not spend much on groceries, because he had everything on his land, including goats' milk.

After three months passed, from the day I was discharged from the military, I was transferred to the Illinois Army inactive reserves for ten years. I went back working at the same pharmaceutical company. I ran the reactor for the baby aspirin and raw materials. After six months I was promoted to second shift foreman.

One day a chemical engineer sent me to the department manager. (This man was to become my worst enemy for the next twenty seven years)! He told me that he was working on a new project with a chemist, and the chemist was not getting good results. I told the engineer that I was not a chemist. I was going to seminars and some courses sponsored by the company. He explained that all I had to do was to follow his written instructions and run the equipment and keep records of temperatures, boiling points, etc. The equipment consisted of an eighteen hundred gallon reactor, a separator, or fractionators' column plus a receiver. Everything was run with high pressure steam. The whole idea was to separate a chemical called cyclohexilamine from the rest of the other chemicals. Everything was working fine for two weeks until I took a sample of the recovered product to the analytical lab. The cyclohexilamine was not one hundred percent. There were traces of the other chemical. The engineer came asked me, "What did you do wrong"?

I answered; "I do not know you tell me".

He replied, "Don't get smart with me".

The department manager called me to his office, he asked me how I was doing, and I said I am doing fine, but this guy expects miracles from me. Then he asked do you have any suggestions for the process? I said, I am not an engineer and I do not know which college this guy graduated from. He laughed and asked what is your suggestion I replied it is very simple. I think we are using too much steam pressure. I do not have to be a chemist to know how molecules react to heat. The traces of the other chemicals in the cyclohexilamine probably jump into the chamber of the cycloid. This guy came at me like a mad bull. Why didn't you talk to me instead of going to the manager? I did not go to the manager he called me into his office. Ok, the manager told me to lower the steam pressure like you said. Eventually he believes you and trusts you. I told the guy; I will run it one more time for you, after that I will ask to be sent back to the baby aspirin production. I ran for two days and took a liter bottle sample from the receiver. Took it to the analytical lab bingo!! It did work. I went back to the previous job as a second shift foreman. While the company brought in a younger chemical operator class A to run the recovery of the cyclohexilamine. Everything was running well on the second shift. I told the operator, I am going for lunch now and when I return, then you go for your lunch. One of my responsibilities was to check the temperatures and all pressure gauges every thirty minutes. Then record them on the batch sheet and write my initials. As I returned from lunch, I heard an explosion (Boom) it was not a fire, it was a giant chemicals shower coming from above. It was boiling chemicals and the worse one, was sodium hydroxide, (NAoH) better known as caustic soda. (They have that product on the market, liquid Plummer or Drano. That chemical will burn your skin in matter of seconds). I was near the alarm box by the entrance of the building. I grabbed the hammer that was hanging by the alarm box. I broke the glass and pulled the alarm. I closed my eyes and went directly into where the operator was. I grabbed him, did an army about face. At the same time there were two guys with fire hoses running water on us. While telling me to walk in a straight line I reached the outside and they grabbed us. They had rubber gloves on. They removed our uniforms and safety shoes. Our skin was coming off. The ambulance was already there waiting for us. They rushed us to Saint Therese Hospital in Waukegan, Illinois. They began to work on us I had burns on my legs, both arms and my face. My eyes were closed shut for the next two months. While I recuperated, I still have scars on my legs and arms, and thanks to the Lord, my face is normal, I only have impairment in my right eye.

I went back to work at same job and only worked six months of the year because of the accident. One day the department manager called me into his office. He said, Hector we need a good operator to work in research and development. This is a great opportunity for you. You will be making more money, and will be taking seminars and courses from time to time. I accepted the challenge and went to work immediately. It was a big difference in equipment size. Reactors were from two gallons to fifty gallons. I organized all the equipment, put some shelving up and marked everything by name and size. I was working with the in-organic section once a week to assist the chemist in charge of the new project. That product is on the market today. This product is injected into the vein of people with blood clot problems. The raw material consisted of the foam collected from urine and (NaoH) sodium hydroxide. This process is called fermentation and smelled like rotten eggs. You could smell the stench miles away. They had a crew of men that went out every day. They placed containers in the naval bases, army camps, taverns and places they could collect the urine. We had two wooden vessels at fifteen hundred gallons each. They each had a stainless steel agitator that would mix the batch of urine. We start adding the sodium hydroxide, also known as caustic soda. When the foam began forming on top, you would then turn off the agitator and let it ferment for sometimes two weeks. We alternated the vessels so we always had foam. After the fermentation was completed we would climb the ladder to the tops of the vessel and collect the foam, sometimes up to four inches of foam. We then proceeded to put the foam in deep stainless steel pans then into a rack on wheels. We would push the rack into a walk in oven and let it dry at a low temperature. Then we would pull the rack out of the oven and run the powder thru a screen. We put the powder in plastic bags and sent them to the production department, to continue the process by adding other chemicals, into a glass lined reactor with a condensator. The vapors would rise up into the condensator. The vapors are cooled down inside the condensator by running cold water thru the condensator jacket. Vapors come out in liquid form and into a receiver, and that is the final product.

I received a telephone call from my oldest daughter as usual. The conversation is always the same my daughter like my two sisters wanted to be a school teacher from kindergarten to high school. She kept perfect grades. When she began her junior year in high school she was sixteen years old. I rewarded her with a convertible Buick skylark. That was in the year nineteen-sixty seven. In the conversation we had today, she made a remark typical of my daughter. She began by saying that her mother was very happy with the grandchildren in the house with her. She continues by saying that we pay for the decisions we make in life. I have to agree with her. She said that I should be aware of the fact that I left the home, and I have to face the consequences. Then she added, one day you are going to come to the pick up your mail and find your Bible on the floor with a bullet in it. I do not understand what she meant with those words. She also mentioned that I was not welcomed back home.

As I always do, after talking to my daughter I said my little prayer. I opened the Bible and my eyes went directly to Corinthians 1 threw 9: I always Thank God for you, because of his grace given you in Christ Jesus. For in him you have enriched in every way in all your speaking and in all your knowledge because our testimony about Christ was confirmed in you. Therefore you do not lack any spiritual gift, as you eagerly wait for our lord Jesus Christ to be revealed. He will keep you strong to the end, so that you will be blameless on the days of our lord Jesus Christ. God, who has called you into fellowship with his son Jesus Christ our lord, is faithful. (Amen). My daughter does not realize how right she is about the bad decisions we make in our lives. I honestly believe that you can change your destiny. We are born sinners, with a purpose for life from the womb of your mother you are sinners.

CHAPTER 2
SELF EXILE

Hilda came home one day and informed my wife that she wanted to get married. My wife became very angry. She told her that she was not going to have a very good future with this person. My wife wanted to send her to my sisters in Puerto Rico. She was to attend the University of Puerto Rico (UPR) along with my niece and my nephew. (Today my nice is a Judge in the Supreme Court in San Juan, Puerto Rico). My nephew is a criminal lawyer with this own practice also in Puerto Rico. My wife finally gave up on her and one day she beat her with one of her shoes. That was the end of all the arguments but not the problems for my beautiful daughter. That was the beginning of hell on earth for my daughter. The Bible is the word of God, I have said this before and I say it again. I have been blessed since I was in my mother's womb! I just glanced at the book of proverbs chapter 4-1, Listen my sons to a father's instruction, pay attention and gain understanding, it will give you sound learning, so do not forsake my teaching. A wise son heeds his father's instruction but a mocker does not listen to rebuke. The day of the wedding arrived, it was the largest wedding ever performed in the area. There were around six hundred fifty invited and non invited guests. We had plenty of food and two musical groups. We did not know where they were going for their honey moon. After the wedding party ended at two in the morning, my wife and I went home to get my pickup truck. We have never seen so many gifts in a wedding. The reason for having so many guests and gifts was because we were long time members of a church. At the time, I was production superintendant at the chemical plant. We put all the gifts in the pickup truck and my wife's Lincoln town car. We were so tired that we went home drove both vehicles into the garage and left them there until the next morning.

In nineteen seventy one our first granddaughter Tracy Lynn was born. What a bundle of joy! Instead of my son-in-law being happy about being a father he began drinking excessively; sometimes he would drink all of his money and did not come home. My daughter had no choice but to go to work. She got a job with the telephone company to support herself and the baby.

My younger daughter knew what she wanted and told us that college was not in her mind. She will graduate from high school and then go to work.

Charlie my son, perhaps my childhood upbringing contributed to the manner I treated him and my family. I really wanted to be a good father and husband and wanted the best for all. God knows that my wife is the only woman that I ever loved and sixty-years later I still love her! To me, my wife is one of the best mothers and grandmothers in the world. She does not believe in discipline, and defines discipline as an act of abuse. Because of the communication advanced systems used these days. You read in the news papers, you hear on television and radio, the activities committed by both parents, sometimes the results is the death of an innocent child. I feel that I was abusive with my discipline, but one cannot see their own misdealing, I understand now!

Last night my nephew Frankie called me from New Jersey. I thank God for Frankie. Besides God, Frankie is my best witness today. Since Frankie turned eighteen years of age and went into the Military, we never lost contact with each other. When his mother passed away in Puerto Rico, I was the only one of the family to be with him. We arranged everything together at the Funeral Home. Frankie is now 58 eight years old and he and his wife procreated two daughters and a son. Like my wife and I. A boy came first and then two daughters. I use to call Frankie, Ralph and my son Charlie the three musketeers. They grew up together and went to school together. To continue talking about the three musketeers is another story!

My career began to move ahead in the year Nineteen sixty one I accepted the job offer from the cosmetic company. I consulted the pastor of the church and family members. The only one that told me that she knew me very well, and I have never been a looser, was my wife, so I went to work at the plant. The manager was an Italian American. We immediately became very good friends. We started running two different products but we only had one building for production, warehouse office and a small lunch room. We also had the analytical lab with only one chemist.

I was the only chemical operator at the time. I was running the detergent for the hair shampoo. Which was very popular at the time This shampoo, was White Rain; they had a commercial on television of twin sisters with long hair. The twin sisters were under the rain each one had a bottle of shampoo and they said. It pours and shines when it rains. All shampoos are produced the same way. They have the same basic ingredients. The water is run thru a six foot column, this is called a deionizer. The column has a resin bed whit a pump from the holding vessel. It recycles from the holding tank and into the deionizer. You start with a high PH, to explain the meaning of (PH); this determines the acidity or alkalinity of a liquid. The range of the (PH), runs from (0-12) neutral are 7.0, anything fewer than seven is considered acid. Take a bottle of coke and check the (PH); you will get a reading of (4.5) that is considered acid. In the other hand, you take any detergent and check the (PH) you should get a reading of 6.7 - 6.9. I do not buy or drink bottled water for many reasons. The only time I drink it is if it is absolutely necessary. When I go and visit my nephew Frankie in Florida, I have no choice. To me, Florida has the worst water in the United States. Florida's water smells like rotten eggs, because it contains a large amount of sulfur dioxide. I was visiting Frankie and every morning after breakfast we would drive by the country side. We would go to the Veterans Administration (VA) Hospital for Frankie's appointments. He was on a motorized wheel chair provided by the VA. Once a week he would go to an acupuncture specialist for his pain management therapy. We would drive by the ocean or stop at the park to walk Buddy, Frankie's dog. We stopped to have some ice cream. We always had a good time. One morning after breakfast, I asked him what the agenda is for today. He replied we are going to buy water at the water plant. We put two five gallons jugs in the pickup truck and away we go. After driving for about twenty minutes we arrived at the water plant. As soon as I entered the building I noticed the number of deionizers in series. This is called ION exchange; they removed the minerals from the water by using sodium hydroxide (NaOH) and hydrochloric acid (HCL) for the last thirty seven years I have been using a carbon filter at home; we get crystal clear water and the cheapest protein you can buy. There was only one operator at the water plant, and he was the owner. I told him that I was familiar with the procedures, and that I had been working for 40 years on a similar procedure. At the time I was seventy-three years old. Frankie just stood by listening. The same day we went looking at Recreational Vehicles (RV) and I was walking alongside his wheel chair. Suddenly his chair hit a low side of the gravel road and down he went. He landed on his left side and he was bleeding from his hands and forearm as he tried to catch himself. I tried to help him up, but refused my help. He said to me, uncle just brings the chair next to me and I will do the rest. He got up and we went inside and again refused help into the building. He asked for a roll of paper towel, went into the men's room, washed his hands and arms. We left the RV site to return home. When we arrived I told his wife what had happened and she replied it isn't the first time that's happened. After visiting Frankie for two weeks, I went home. The following Monday, I went back to work. The company with the main plant in Saint Paul Minnesota, purchased two hundred twenty acres of farm land for future expansion. We were making the detergent early Monday morning. The plant manager came to me and said, Hector they called me from Saint Paul. They are way behind with the demand for the white rain shampoo. Do you have any suggestions? At the time I was making two thousand gallons of detergent in eight hour shifts. We were filling by gravity fiber lined drums on pallets and the warehouse forklift operator would take the completed drums and put them on the tractor trailer. We already had a six thousand gallon stainless steel receiver with huge pumps. I advised the manager, we needed to hire two chemical operators immediately. I will run two shifts until the operators are ready to take over. He interviewed ten operators, and picked two of them. He sent them to me with the application. I showed them the equipment the pumps, reactors, pressure steam gauges and so forth. I called the manager and told him, I will begin training them tomorrow one person for the day shift and the other for the second shift. I trained the two operators for the next three weeks. Instead of drumming the detergent, we pumped three batches into the six thousand vessels, and from the vessel into a tanker truck outside and then they were on the way to Saint Paul. After three weeks of training we began working three shifts six days a week.

I was promoted to production supervisor with a big increase in salary, and given the keys for the front gate and the front door to the plant. Saint Paul began making the blue dye for the paper mate pens. We had to produce the raw material for them. One year later, they began the hair spray (Tony) we had to make the resin that was the main ingredient. Each time we added a new product. We had to hire and train more operators, it was too much work for the team we had. We had to promote three operators to shift supervisors. We kept adding more buildings and more products. My good friend the manager had to hire an engineer with a Masters degree in chemistry to run the development department. We got acquainted immediately. He and his wife were very humble Christian people. Slowly but steady the company kept growing and I kept growing with it. We hired twelve more chemical operators, to be trained for all three shifts. The chemist in charge of the raw materials for the hot shave foam was having a hard time in the production area. He was not getting a product that passed the analysis of the control lab. I said to him, you know very well that when you run those tiny reactors and condensation that look like flamingo legs, in the laboratory. You are running litters and milliliters. You get good results in the lab. You grab your calculator, ruler and you figure out the amount of material we need for production. Most of the time it works! Now going to college is very important to learn the theory and obtain a degree but my education was my past experience. I remember during my childhood, I was in the boys scouts of America. The scout master was a young man, twenty three years old. He graduated from the University of Puerto Rico with a Bachelors Degree in Education. He was also a Second Lieutenant with the Reserve Officers Training Corps (ROTC). He was drafted when the Korean War began. Right after basic training he was commissioned as a Second Lieutenant. He was the platoon leader and sent to Korea with the 65thh Infantry Army Battalion, attached to the 3rd Army Division. Frankie my nephew's grandfather was killed while serving in France. The 65th Infantry was attached to the Seventh Army Division in World War II. This Battalion has been one hundred percent of Puerto Rican natives, since the First World War in 1917. The Battalion was sent to Korea in 1950, that was five years after the end of the Second World War They had so many casualties that they had to activate the 295th Infantry to replace them due to the casualties. This is where my scout master the Second Lieutenant was attached. They were in South Korea for only two weeks, then the Platoon was sent on a reconnaissance patrol threw an open field. When on a patrol you keep distance between soldiers in two columns. The platoon leader walks in front and the platoon sergeant in the rear. The Chinese and North Koreans were hiding in the trenches dug into the ground. They open fire killing the Platoon leader instantly. The platoon sergeant took over and immediately returned fire with thirty caliber machine guns and rifles. The radio man gave the mayday signal and six helicopters came with machine guns and killed the enemy. The Platoon Sergeant was awarded with a field commission and promoted to platoon leader. My point is, that I was trying to emphasize to the chemist at work that you do not have to hold a college degree to obtain a promotion. I always keep in mind that the great President Abraham Lincoln was self educated. After talking to the chemist about my previous experiences with certain chemicals, he agreed to begin with temperature changes.

CHAPTER 3
ENJOYING WORK

We made the first batch and barely passed the analysis of quality control. The name of the material was (Barby). We called it Barby, because it was a form of barbiturates. They added this material to the shaving foam at the main plant. This ingredient when you squeeze the foam onto the palm of your hand it would gets very warm. With my thirty five years of working with chemicals. I have learned many things; one example is at home and in the restaurants. I have to cook and sometimes, experiment with different types of foods. My specialty is chicken soup or fish soup. When cooking the soup it has to be on weekends, the whole family is invited. My youngest daughter that lives one block away from us, always tells me, daddy, I cook the soup like you taught me. But the soup is never the same. I use to buy once a week a roasted chicken at the same place for about two years. One day my wife said to me, go and buy a roasted chicken while making a tossed salad and garlic bread, for tonight's dinner. I drove my pickup truck to the chicken place ten minutes away, I drove home with my delicious hot chicken. My wife cut it up and took a small bite and asked, where you bought this chicken, I replied I bought it at the same place we always buy it. She handed me a piece and said, try it. I put it to my mouth, she was right it had a different taste, but we ate it any way, chicken is a poor man's steak. The next day I went to the same business and asked the owner, did you still have the Spanish cook? He answered; no you are not the only person that has asked that question today. The Hispanic cook quit two weeks ago. Now I have an oriental cook. I gave him a big smile went home and told my wife. My point again is you can take different cooks give them the same equipment same ingredients and the results will not be the same quality. They kept me working for the next three months with the barbiturate. The main plant was using the material faster than producing it. For all chemicals you make, the operator has a batch sheet with the instructions and procedures to follow. You start with batch numbers and date. Raw materials name amounts and serial number of each material. You have a temperature recorder installed on top of the reactor. This recorder will record the temperature of the batch in degree centigrade. (DC). the way it works, is very simple. All reactors are either glass lined or stainless steel. They come with an agitator, baffles and a permanent glass or stainless steel vertical pipe inside the reactor. This pipe is called the WELL for the thermocouple that runs from the recording temperature instrument and into the WELL. When training the chemical operators, it is required that you read the companies manuals and instruction. We continued making Barby for the next three months. With my continued advancements, I was able to buy my first motor home, to go on vacations with my wife and two year old grandson. We took him to the Elvis Presley mansion two times. Bought him a little guitar and he started imitating Elvis and everywhere we went he would carry his guitar.

I told the manager of the Plant that I would like to take my three weeks' vacation, to travel in my motor home to, Key West, Florida to go deep sea fishing on a Charter boat. He replied, "Hector you more than anyone else deserve to go on a vacation. You have never missed a day of work, never get sick, and you have done so much for the company. Everyone at the Saint Paul Plan know you by name! I would like to surprise you; he grabbed the phone and called the secretary in the front lobby. He asked the secretary, did you make the reservations for Hector?"

She replied yes, he read the information to me! Hector you leave Monday from Chicago, Illinois to Saint Paul, Minnesota and returning on Thursday.

When I arrived at the airport at Saint Paul, a company chauffeur picked me up at the airport and took me to the hotel. The chauffeur said that he would pick me up at 7:00 a. m. the next day and take me to the main Plant. I was so excited about this venture that I didn't get much sleep that night, because I was thinking how I should dress, so I decided that morning to dress up in a white shirt, black pants, black shoes and a red tie. The chauffeur was punctual the next morning. To my surprise he exited the vehicle and opened the back door so I could enter the back seat. I requested to ride in the front seat because I would feel more comfortable. I told him that I was in the back seat from the airport because I thought he was a taxi driver. He laughed and replied, sir this is the company policy toward their guests. That is wonderful but I only apply the company policy and rules while at work. You know, when you are in the military you are taught to be professional, twenty-four seven. Everywhere you go you represent your country and are indoctrinated, that's what the military teaches you.

We arrived at the Minnesota plant and walked to the cafeteria. There were four gentlemen dressed in black just like me. They were four managers from four different departments, Production quality control, research and development and shipping. We had a very good breakfast and we were taken on a tour of the company. We started at the packing lines, were the conveyor belts are running slow but steady. There was a long line of women standing up with white uniforms, hair nets and gloves. They filled the cardboard boxes with the product. At the end of the conveyor belt, were men stacking the boxes on pallets and fork lifted into the warehouse. We stopped the tour at noon and went for lunch. We finished the day with a movie and conference of a branch of the company which was being constructed in South America. After the tour the chauffeur drove me back to the hotel at 4:00 p. m. That night I was very impressed with the opportunity to visit this company, which made me very relaxed. At the hotel I went downstairs to the bar restaurant. A male waiter took me to a table and placed the menu for the particular day in front of me. I ordered a bottle of beer and the lobster dinner. About ten minutes passed and I see this beautiful blonde walking thru the door. She did not wait for the usher to bring her to the table. She sat down right across from where I was seating. I noticed that without her ordering, the waiter brought her a cocktail. I was wondering is she a regular customer. Then all of a sudden like if God was speaking to me, I thought, this must be a trap someone is testing me to question my integrity. I ate my dinner in a hurry and she got up from her table. She came over to me and asked, are you passing by, I answered yes, she replied, I was observing your beautiful curly black hair and long sideburns. You must be Hispanic, yes, I replied, and then I called the waiter to add twenty percent to the ticket. That was the maximum tip allowed by the company. She wished me good luck, and to have a good trip. I returned to my room, I watched boxing and then went to sleep.

Next day was my last tour of the Plant. The chauffeur picked me up on time as usual. As we arrived at the Plant I went to the cafeteria to have breakfast. The last part of the tour consisted of the raw material we produced at the North Chicago Branch. They stressed how important it was to have a good quality product. At noon we went to the cafeteria for lunch. We were talking and laughing, and I kidded the others that I was the youngest of the group. We laughed! All of the sudden the girl that was seated across from me at dinner last night entered the cafeteria with a tray of food. She sat down with two other females at the same table. One of the guys said, that she goes there all the time especially on weekends. Her oldest brother is the manager of the hotel. She is twenty seven years old and single. She is working for quality control. Her time is getting close for being an "old maid". She is looking for a mature man to get married. Inside, I smiled and figured out the whole situation.

I returned home and went back to work the following Monday. My boss called me to his office and informed me that he was planning to retire in two years. I continued working as the production supervisor. One year passed and he called me to his office. He said, Hector I am going to South America for the opening of the new branch. The next in line to replace me is Ed and he needs you here. Ed was the deployment engineer. He and I worked well together. My boss went to South America and came back in three weeks. I was training a class (A) operator in the Barby building. He came to me and said, Hector I wish you were with me in South America, everybody would come to me speaking Spanish. My boss was American Italian; he was very dark and three inches shorter than I.

When he had six months left before his retirement, he informed me that Ed the next Plant manager wanted me to be the production superintendant. He was going to build an office for me in the production area. He said to me Hector, I received a personal letter from South America in Spanish, and can you translate it for me. He handed the letter to me; I read the letter to myself and began to laugh. Ed wanted to know what was wrong. I replied are you certain you want me to tell you what this lady has written? Ed replied yes, okay, here we go.

Dear Lover, just a few lines to thank you for the wonderful time you gave me during the two nights at the Copacabana Hotel. No one ever loved me like you did. That's enough he said, I had too many martinis; I am going to burn this letter right now! Promise you are not going to mention this to anyone. I have never mentioned this until now. Like the pharmaceutical company in North Chicago. I am the first Puerto Rican national to be hired at the cosmetic company. I finally took my three weeks' vacation.

My wife and I drove the motor home to Key West, FL. This was in the year 1972 in early December. When we left early Monday morning it was snowing and very cold. We rose early in the morning and began our trip south on Highway 65. We drove thirty five miles and stopped at the next town to eat breakfast and gas up the RV. Went into the restaurant and ordered the largest southern breakfast for me and the smallest for my wife. We began heading south and it stayed cold until we passed Atlanta, GA. We arrived to north Florida and began to see the hibiscus and the flowers. Immediately our moods changed and we felt that joy inside. After arriving to Florida, we were getting tired of the long drive; we pulled into a (RV) recreational vehicle park. The hoses of the RV were hooked up along with the electricity. While my wife took a shower, I watched the news in the black and white thirteen inch Television. My wife has never been a big eater but she likes red meat. We had steak and pork chops prepared in the motor home refrigerator. We also had a generator in the rear of the motor home. We ate a steak sandwich and a can of vegetable soup. After we ate we retired for the night. Before going to bed I always prepare a place for my firearm in the camper for protection of my family and me. In the camper are a .357 magnum pistol and a bolt action rifle with a 10 round magazine. I purchased the rifle at an old small Sears Roebuck store on Washington Street in Wakegan, IL. I was a member of a gun club in Illinois and Puerto Rico. This rifle is 49 years old in 2010. It is perfectly clean and you can read on the barrel the serial numbers and the name Sears and Roebuck Company. The southern big breakfast cost $1.10 and the small breakfast $0.60 cents, with all the coffee you can drink. We drove all the way to Homestead, FL in South Dade County. At the time it was all farm land it was beautiful. Miles and miles of vegetables, oranges, grapefruits, avocados, it looked like a green ocean without an end. We stayed in Homestead in an old farm with no electricity or running water. The old man said, you can stay it is $3.00 a day. Thank God we still had the reserve fresh water tank full. My wife was afraid to stay there overnight. It was getting late and I did not like to drive at night. I told my wife, let's rest until daylight and then leave early morning. I put the .357 magnum in my waist belt and went outside to turn on the generator. From out of nowhere, this young farmer starts approaching towards me with a machete. He was about fifteen feet away from me and he said howdy. I answered do not come any closer, because I am going to get nervous. He replied that's a nice piece (gun) in your belt. I replied and I know how to use it if necessary. He said you have a good night. As soon as he left, I turned off the generator and told my wife that we were leaving. She was very happy to hear that. I took highway US 1 south and drove to less than an hour. We found a rest area where there were RV's and RV overnight parking. We parked there and I asked my wife why, were you afraid at the first stop? She replied I wasn't scared for us; I was scared that you would not hesitate to use your gun!

We rose early the next morning with the noise of the tractor trailer engines roar. Ate a good breakfast at the rest area and continued on US 1. We arrived to Key West in the afternoon and made reservations for the next day's charter boat. We boarded the charter boat and asked the captain. What are those people doing seating on the benches with five gallons empty buckets? He answered they are retired and when the tourist catch the fish and do not want them they put the fish in the buckets. We went out into the ocean about eight miles out. For a moment I thought we were in Cuban waters. We stopped at this area where the fish finder located a large shoal of fish. They lowered the anchor and the captain came down with two assistants. They supplied the fish rods and hook up the bait for each person. After all the rods were ready, the Captain said, we have a contest for the largest fish caught. If you want to participate it will cost $3.00 per person and the winner takes all the money. I gave him $6.00 for my wife and I and twenty more people joined the contest. The Captain said get ready to cast out on my signal. GO! He yelled and everybody casted out and as soon as the bait hit the water all the lines began pulling fish onto the boat. Everybody began yelling and screaming. Any fish under two pounds was thrown back into the sea. Unbelievable, we had never seen so many fish before. The Captain and the helpers could not keep up with removing the fish from the hooks, and re-baiting the fishing rods. One guy next to me landed a six pound and four ounces red snapper almost immediately. I pulled in a five and half pound snapper. My wife was next to me and I noticed that her line was running away from her. I began yelling at her to do it on her own because I had another fish on my line. She was having a hard time with the fish because it was a big one. Finally one of the boat hands came to her rescue. She caught the biggest fish of the trip, a red snapper eight pounds and three ounces. She won the money from the pot. We started heading back to shore. The ocean began getting rough. The vessel was rocking up and down and I had to grab my wife and sit her down. She almost vomited all over me. We finally arrived back to shore. My wife said to me this is my first and last fishing trip! She has never been fishing again to date! We left the pier and drove back north to Miami.

We saw a sign for (KOA) Campground followed the directions and it took us to the Krome Avenue southwest Dade County. We arrived at the camp ground and checked in. They had a swimming pool, electricity, water and sewer. Actually it was well water and septic tank. I had seven days left of my three weeks' vacation. We liked this camp ground because it was winter time and there were plenty of campers from the state of Illinois. We agreed to stay at the KOA Camp Ground four days. The city of Miami was not far from where we were staying. There was a large concentration of Cubans and Puerto Ricans in Miami. When I was a kid, I heard people say; Cuba and Puerto Rico are the two wings of a bird. They receive flowers and bullets in the same heart. They had Bodegas (little stores) that sold all kinds of Latino produce. My wife wanted to buy Bacalao (salt dry fish); enough for the family and friends back home. In the 1960's we would drive to Chicago, Illinois to buy the Latino products and were much more expensive, than in Miami. From the plantations we could purchase for $1.00 a big bag of large avocado's not too far from where we were camping. We saw a big sign that said acres for sale. At the time we did not have cellular's like nowadays, my wife wrote the telephone number of the realtor and we returned to the camp site. From the camp-ground telephones, we called the realtor. The realtor agreed to pick us up at the camp site because he had to drive the same route. We drove about for 10 minutes to the lots.

The lots were segregated by numbers and street names. (You were not allowed to build a house in less than one and a half acres, because of the contamination of the well waters with the septic fields). We decided for a corner lot because it was very level and higher than the rest of the lots. The price of each lot was six thousand nine hundred dollars. The corner lot was another thousand dollars. We wrote a check and went to the Realtors' office to sign the contract. The contract was for seventh thousand nine hundred dollars. We applied a thousand dollar down payment, with three hundred and fifty a month for one year registered check with no interest.

On Friday early morning we left so we could beat the traffic, we started driving back to Waukegan, Illinois. I had to be back to work on Monday morning. In the afternoon we arrived in Atlanta, Georgia there was heavy traffic. I did not stop and continued to Chattanooga, Tennessee, I would have continued but my wife was getting restless. We spotted a KOA Camp Ground and pulled in to stay for the night. The next morning we started driving north again, when we arrived to Kentucky, we started feeling the cold weather, not like in Florida. We parked at a rest stop for eight hours, at three o'clock in the morning I woke up and started driving my wife was still sleeping. When she woke up she said I was crazy for getting up so early. We continued driving and arrived back early Sunday morning and back to shoveling snow. The worse part of the trip was going thru Chicago and Atlanta, GA.

Back to work Monday morning, as I entered the production area, there was my new office fully equipped. My boss came into my office with the new engineer, which he had hired. I froze and my boss asked, what's wrong Hector? I said ask him! Then they left. This new engineer was the person that I had a problem with at the pharmaceutical company and he got fired. The boss came back and told me that he knew me from the previous job. I told the boss that this guy was a racist and got fired from the pharmaceutical company. The boss replied, Hector you have nothing to worry about. I am going to retire in six month. Ed and I already have planned for the future of the company. There are two more buildings to be built within the next three years. Your friend the new engineer will be in charge of the project and had nothing to do with your job.

The day came for my good boss to retire. We had a retirement party on a Saturday night at the Holiday Inn. All the spouses were invited. Before the dinner was served, the boss stood up and announced, beginning on Monday, Ed will be the new plant manager. Fred (new engineer) will take over Ed's position. Also Hector will be promoted to the production superintendant. We had two groups of music playing and we were dancing having a good time. Everyone was drinking martinis, manhattans and all kinds of liquors. I usually am a beer drinker and my wife seldom drinks any liquor, until she turned fifty years young. Everyone began to get tipsy and Fred's wife came to the table and sat down with us. She began the conversation by saying what a beautiful couple we were. She told my wife that she looked so young; my wife didn't understand what she was saying because of her heavy southern accent. She was getting all wound up and began speaking about her personal life. She told us that she had two teenage children from a previous marriage, a seventeen year old daughter, and a nineteen year old son. She said that Fred had a son in college and he was the only child from his previous marriage. Finally she stopped talking, my wife was just listening. The lady didn't know that my wife was from a humble home, where you do not talk about your personal life with strangers. It was getting uncomfortable for my wife, so around 11:00 p. m. we left and went home.

Monday morning as usual my wife and I had to go to work. My wife has a job at a pharmaceutical company Abbot Laboratories in North Chicago where she worked for ten years. At this time the company had five thousand employees and a large payroll. My wife had a very responsible job, with the quality control department. One day she went to a department meeting and a supervisor saw her last name on her white jacket. He said, I know that name, are you related to Hector? She replied, yes he is my husband. He told my wife that he heard a lot about me and that I had a perfect attendance record. He also said to tell me that research and development would take me back any time.

Now that my boss and friend were retired, Ed the plant manager gave me more responsibilities. Beside's going around the plant every hour and making sure that everything was running normal. The work at the desk was tedious; we had to write everything, not like now with computers. I also had to use a calculator constantly. The chemicals operators would bring the batch sheets and drop them on my desk. The paperwork was for all three shifts. I had to check the amount of raw material using the signature and batch numbers. The final amounts of product by gallons and pounds. The work was piling up. I would take the paperwork home to complete the reports, especially at the end of the month. I would complete the report at home in order to meet monthly deadline for the main office in Chicago, IL. Three months passed and everything was running smoothly. There was a big pond next to the boiler house; we used steam to run the whole plant. It looked like this pond was manmade. They had all kinds of animals at this farm, before the company purchased it from a polish man named George. The deal was that he would live at the farm house with his mother and two cows, dogs and goats. He was to be paid minimum wages to serve as the watchman for the plant. At the time I sold my house and purchased a new one... I asked for two days off in order to move my household. My wife and I checked into a motel 20 miles from the company, so I had to notify the company secretary with a point of contact because I was always on call. Early the next day, someone was knocking on the door of the motel. One of the operators told me they needed me at the plant. I asked what is wrong. He replied the maintenance man was electrocuted. We drove to work in less time than usual. When I arrived at the plant Ed with tears in his eyes told me if you would have been here this wouldn't have happened it was an accident. Fred the engineer of the new construction wanted to pump the water out of the pond and then fill it with dirt, for a new building. The maintenance man a retire Navy Chief survivor of Pearl Harbor, Hawaii, and his helper took a two hundred twenty volt from the centrifugal pump outside by the pond. The engineer was supervising them. They hooked a three inch hose to the inlet of the pump. They proceeded with another tree inches of hose to the outlet. The engineer plugged the electrical cord into the two hundred twenty volt outlet. The pump had a manual switch type handle. The maintenance man was standing in a puddle of water. When he grabbed the switch to turn the pump on, there were a lot of sparks and his whole body began shaking. The helper grabbed a piece of lumber and tried to push him away from the pump. The engineer was standing there staring stun by the event. The helper finally unplugged the electrical cord from the outlet, it was too late. When the police and fire department arrived the body was laying on the ground completely with the color purple. I looked at the pump and noticed that the negative wire was connected improperly. The pump was mounted on a steel frame cart with four steel wheels and the ground was soaking wet and he had steel toed shoes on. The ground wire inside the electrical box by the pump switch was connected where the positive was supposed to be. The positive (live) wire was connected to the body of the pump and the steel made it a perfect electric chair. We discarded the pump because the motor burned out completely.

The deceased and his wife were our very good friends. I went to talk to her and she was very devastated. She was drinking Vodka with grapefruit juice. She began crying and gave me a bottle of beer. She said, Hector I know that somebody wanted to kill him. I cannot believe that he rigged that pump; you know he was a professional electrician. She kept drinking and talking, and finally said, my life has been a disaster. He was my third husband and my three husbands were Navy men. They were the best of friends; they were in Pearl Harbor during the Japanese attack, that's where my first husband died in 1942. Then married my second husband, and he died in Korea in 1950 in a helicopter crash. In 1955 I married my third and last husband. She was crying so hard, that I could not stand it any longer and I began crying with her. She looked at me and said I have more money than I can spend in a life time. She was getting a half million from the company plus she already had pension and life insurance from the previous marriages. She told me that she did not have children, and all she was now was a chronic alcoholic. I started to leave and she said Hector my husband has a collection of movie reels and projectors from the Second World War downstairs in the basement at my house. I do not know what to do with them, if you want them, take them with you. I walked down to the basement and the first thing I saw was two big cages with two big monkeys. Army issued (OD) thirty caliber ammunition boxes. A wall with shelves neatly stacked with movies and projectors. They all were and marked property of the United States Army. As soon as I started touching the movies the two monkeys went wild and crazy. They began shaking the cages and showing their teeth. I went upstairs and told the widow that I didn't want the projectors or movies. I left her and went home. Three months later a neighbor found her dead in the living room of her house in 1973. I have always wondered if she knew more about her husband's death than she led on.

CHAPTER 4
YOUNG & REBELLIOUS

In 1974 my youngest daughter decided to get married. On October 4th, 1974 my son Charlie was in a car accident and passed. That was the worst day of my life, he was rebellious but still he was my son. I was acting strong so my wife could have my shoulder to cry on! Instead she took the accident as if I didn't care. This has never stopped; my wife still thinks it was my fault! I leave this in God's hands. In 1975 my daughter gave birth to my grandson Justin. He resembles my son Charlie and how much they look alike.

The last time I seen my oldest brother was in 1955, I say this because I always correspond with my sisters in Puerto Rico. By brother was retired from the Army and opened a television repair shop. He worked in the shop four six years and things were not going too well. He sold the shop and went to work at a junior college teaching electronics. He wrote me a letter and asked if I could help one of my sons. My nephew was twenty three years old. He married and his wife was 6 years his senior and they had a son. I rented a one bedroom apartment and purchased the necessary furniture for them to start a residence. They flew from Puerto Rico to O'Hare International Airport Chicago Illinois, picked them up and took them to the apartment. The language was no problem because everyone in my family attended bi-lingual schools. I spoke to Ed, my supervisor at work and asked him to hire and allow me to train my nephew. He agreed and the following Monday he started working. He learned very fast and he liked the job. When he received his first check, he replied I have never seen so much money before.

After my oldest daughter married the same man for the third time, she approached me and asked, daddy can you help my husband get a job? I replied you know that he dropped out of high school. The only way he can get a job with me is if you help him fill out the application. I hope he doesn't let me down. I had a good talk with her husband, and explained to him that my reputation was on the line with this company. After he was hired I trained him to be an operator's helper for 90 days. I also let him know that if he came to work with alcohol on his breath or hangover that would be a reason to be dismissed immediately. After he completed the ninety days probation period he was transferred to chemical operator. The irony of all was that even without a good formal education he kept learning and retaining all the information. My daughter was very happy now that he had a steady paying job. The company provided free health care insurance for the family and a good life insurance. One year passed when my good friend the previous manager came to visit the plant. As he arrived and I saw him, he said to me in Italian "bon giorno frattelo" good day brother. He gave me a big hug and told me I remember what you told me when we hired Fred. He said Hector remember you told me he was pretty dangerous. Anyways let's talk about what I came here for, you remember the owner of the fiber glass company in Chicago? I replied yes! When you started working with me in 1961 he was the one that built all the holding tanks and vent lines. He called me on Saturday and told me that he has a contract for two months in Barceloneta, Puerto Rico. This new company is going to make all the plastic containers for Puerto Rico and the Virgin Islands. He wanted to know if you would be willing to go with his son and install a hot air dryer. His son is 32 years old and a bachelor. I told Cass my ex-supervisor; I would like to go, but what about Ed the plant manager. I talked to him already and he has no objection. I have been noticing for the last six months that Ed, Fred and Bob and one of the analytical lab chemists were good drinking and poker buddies. One Sunday morning before departing to Puerto Rico the owner of the fiber glass company called me at home, he said Hector I would like to meet you at the Holiday Inn in Waukegan, Illinois. I replied yes, the one on Green Bay Road its only ten minutes from my residence. We met before noon, went into the Bar Restaurant and sat at a corner table. I pulled a chair to the wall and faced him. He asked you always do that, I replied yes, since I was 12 years old because a boy sitting behind me hit me with a ruler. He laughed and began speaking.

Hector I am very pleased that you are going to Puerto Rico with my son, he is an industrial engineer. He is a good son and a good worker. This is his first trip to San Juan and you know how it is in the tourist area twenty four hours a day. My son is still single because he doesn't know how to handle women. You will have to keep an eye on him especially on the weekends. By the way the equipment and parts for the air dryer are already in the Port of embarkation in Miami, Florida. When you arrive in San Juan, go to the docks and check for the shipments arrival. My son will be with you at all times. Your job is to translate for my son.

We arrived in San Juan and rented a Chevrolet Malibu for the next two months. We went to El Condado a tourist area and rented a two room guest house with kitchenette and living room area. The Plant where we were going to install the dryer was around two and a half hours from San Juan. It was located in the same area that Abbot Laboratories had a plant with a three thousand employees on their payroll. This is the pharmaceutical company that I worked for ten years in the early fifties. My oldest nephew Max was the Project Superintendant at this Plant in Puerto Rico. He earned a (PHD) in industrial engineering. We drove to Barceloneta to check the area and hire four temporary workers. We needed a fork lift, truck and we borrowed one from the ware house already established. We hired four workers and they only spoke Spanish, one of them asked me, where are you from? I told the man that I was Puerto Rican and I was born in San Juan. My partner didn't know what was going on. He said I heard the word Gringo and then he laughed and made a remark, you don't really look like a Puerto Rican. We went to check out the building where the air dryer was to be installed. The warehouse provided us with a folding table for the blue prints. This was a huge hair dryer that I had never seen before. In the first four days we marked and drilled all the holes on the concrete floor according to the blue print specifications. We were going to use lead anchors with stainless steel bolts. We received a telephone call from the owner; the father of my partner. He was calling from Chicago, and informed us that the dryer was in San Juan in the Shipyard. We drove to San Juan to pick up the dryer, but first we had to go to the Customs office to pay the receiving taxes as required by the Common Wealth of Puerto Rico. We went to the ship yard and identified the three trailer trucks with the equipment. We hired an independent tractor trailer hauler right there by the docks. He was to take one trailer at a time for the next three days to the plant in Barceloneta. When the trailers arrived at the Plant we started working immediately. The engineer would explain to me according to the blue prints. Then I personally operated the fork lift moving the structure into place which was the foundation for the dryer. The four workers lined up the sections and bolted them with stainless steel bolts. The first four weeks went beautiful until my partner met a gorgeous long black hair hooker in the Condado area in San Juan. We went to see a show that came from Las Vegas. She walked past us and bumped into him. She said, excuse me sir, he said its okay, I explained to him that she was a prostitute. He asked how do you know? It's simple look at the way she is dressed. Her makeup is very heavy out of proportion, and the flower on the side of her hair means that she is available. After sitting and drinking four rum and coke's (Cuba Libre) he was more confident. He looked very mellow and confident. She was sitting with another girl by a table next to the Bar. He stood up and asked her to dance. When they finished dancing he joined the two girls at their table. He waved at me to join him at the girls table. I grabbed his drink and my beer and joined them. I told him lets go to the men's room, he replied good idea. I told him, you never leave your drink unattended that's why I drink beer in the bottle and if the waiter brings it to the table I tell him to open the beer at the table. I also told him that a high cost prostitute charges you a large amount of money. She either has a gigolo, a bartender to put drugs in her clients drink or the waiter. You do not go with her to any place she chooses. We went back to the table and I began to speak Spanish with them. My Partner told me speak English so I understand what you all are saying. I had a reason for talking to the girls in Spanish to explain that I was Puerto Rican so do not take advantage of my co-worker. Well my partner kept talking to the girls and let them know where we were staying. Every weekend they had wild parties at the guest house. The owner was a middle aged new-yor-Rican woman and she provided the Cuban sandwiches, but you had to pay very high prices for the drinks. That night my partner took the gorgeous black haired lady to his room and she spent the night with him. The next morning Saturday the telephone rang at 9:00 a.m. I answered and it was his father the boss. I told him that his son was taking a shower. I didn't mention anything about the gorgeous girl staying with him. I told him that the job was going very well and if he allows us to work on Saturday, we should be able to complete the work in six weeks. He agreed with me and told me to have his son return his call. My partner got up with his lady friend around 9:30 a.m. and told him to call his father. He replied that he was going to take his lady friend to breakfast and that he would call his father after he gets back. He came back around 6:00 p.m. and the guest house manager was waiting for him. He told my partner that we were not allowed to have people stay overnight at the guest house. He told me that the girl took him shopping to Old San Juan. He called his father and when he hung up the phone, he gave me a very mean look. I asked him what's wrong; he replied a four letter word. I told him by getting angry at me it was not going to help, I told his father the truth about working on Saturdays. The contract is to have the dryer operations within two months. My partner calmed down and apologized for saying the bad word. He said to me that he wasn't in a hurry to go back to Chicago. I like that girl very much and would not mind taking her with me to Chicago. I said to him, you are very well educated you are 34 years old and the only child of well to do parents! That is my biggest problem that I have never been married because of my parents, especially my mother, I had a very nice girl friend in college. We dated for the last three years of school. We met at her parents and they accepted me. I took her to meet my parents because we were going to be engaged. When I asked her to go with me to pick up the engagement ring, she changed her mind and broke off with me. I was devastated and two years later the same thing happened with another girl. I began thinking about what his father said to me at the Holiday Inn back in Illinois. We went to work on Monday and he was very quiet all day. We agreed to work on Saturday's. Friday night around 7:00 p.m. he told me he was going to the Hilton Hotel Casino, I told him that I was staying at the guest house, because we had to get up early and go to work. I went to bed early but the loud music and the people coming from downstairs kept me awake. Finally at two in the morning the party was over and I fell asleep. I woke up at 6:00 a.m. as my partner walked in. I asked him, did you win any money at the casino? He replied I am too tired to go to work. I told him we are going to work and I will drive so you can get some sleep. He replied since when did you start giving me orders! I replied do you want me to call your father? He said alright you win, he handed me the car keys and he slept the whole trip back to the Plant. That night when we went back to the guest house he took a shower and laid down in the living room couch in a matter of seconds he fell asleep. Thank God it was Saturday night and there wasn't any party at the guest house. The owner and the manager of the guest house went to a friend's wedding. The telephone rang I answered and it was the Boss from Chicago. He asked for his son, I told him that he was asleep. So early, he replied. Then he informed me that he was flying to San Juan the next day on Sunday. He told me that he had a rental car waiting for him at the airport, and he had reservations at the Hilton Hotel. He arrived at Isla Verde Airport and drove to the guest house. It was 3:30 p.m. His son and I were playing pool in the recreation room of the guest house. What I did not know was that his son already talked to his mother about his girlfriend. The Boss said, Hector I will pick you up tomorrow morning. He took his son with him and that was the last time I saw him.

Monday morning the boss picked me up early. On the way to work he was very quiet. I asked him where is my partner; all he said was your partner is flying back to Chicago this afternoon. He has to take care of the shop. We drove every day the same route, highway number two. We passed the city of Bayamon every day. I had friends in that city that lived in Illinois for many years. I told the boss that I did not like to stay at the guest house. The only reason I stayed there was because he wanted me to be with his son. My friend in Bayamon city owned a hardware store right by the highway. He and his wife had 3 children; they lived close to me in Illinois. My boss agreed to let me stay in Bayamon. After work he dropped me off at the hardware store. I was glad that he agreed to let me visit my friends. They were very happy to see me and invited me to stay with them. We knew each other very well because we were members of the same club. I was the founder of the Scholarship Fund and president and he was the treasurer for three years. We had various activities to collect funds to help the Hispanic students obtain a college education. My friend and his wife lived and owned a two story all concrete home. She worked as a nurse at a nearby hospital the boss told me Hector you are right we can complete the job in six weeks. I will give you credit for the two month contract. Well we finished the dryer and he went back to Chicago. I stayed with my friends for the next two weeks in Bayamon, Puerto Rico. They gave me a spacious bedroom next to a huge back porch on the second floor. Every morning I would have breakfast and read the newspaper in the back porch. It rained everyday in Bayamon. The people of Puerto Rico baptized Bayamon as the wash bowl of the sky because it rains so much. The last weekend that I spent with my friends, they roasted a young pig, some neighbors came to help and participated in the cook out. They built a pit in the back yard, put charcoal and wood in the bottom of the pit. They light it up and when the flame dies out, they put the pig in the center of the pit hooked on a long steel rod. Then two men turn the rod for long hours until the pig is done. The party lasted until 10:00 p.m. I went to bed because the next day Sunday, I had to catch my flight to return to Chicago, Illinois. I arrived in Chicago Sunday at one thirty in the afternoon and my wife and her brother were waiting for me. Early Monday morning I returned to work and was sitting in my office and 10 minutes later my replacement while I was working in Puerto Rico came into the office. I greeted him good morning, he didn't reply! About an hour later, Ed the manager came to the office, he seemed very happy to see me. With a big smile he welcomed me. He said that the son of the owner of the fiber glass company came to repair a receiver and told him that I was a very dedicated responsible person. The chemical operators wanted to form a bowling team to play in the winter league. I told them that I have never bowled. They insisted and I join them. We were sponsored by the company and to my surprise Ed joined the team. The project engineer (my rival) and his buddy my successor kept on playing cards and drinking binges. I purchased bowling shoes and sixteen pound bowling ball. We were scheduled to play on Friday nights. I went early with my neighbor to take practice shots. We began the competition and my first game was the lowest of the whole league. We kept on playing every Friday and every game I would play better and better. As a team we reached the finals I was bowling a perfect game! The pressure was only on me. I had nine strikes in a row. There were about thirty people behind me. They were standing and yelling rooting for me. I prepared and took aim and let go of the ball. I missed the last frame strike and ended with a two hundred and ninety seven game. After the winter season was over I was given a trophy for the most improved average and highest score.

Everything was going well at work. We used chlorosulfonic acid that was delivered in special lined fifty five gallon drums. These drums weighed seven hundred pounds when full. We kept them outside because this acid is very dangerous, when it comes in contact with water; we had an all concrete ventilated building to keep them in. We used a mixture of fatty acid. This fatty acid is coconut oil processed in form of lard. It is delivered to us in drums and is a solid; we place the drums on top of steam radiators. Covered them with a canvas, early the next morning they are liquefied. We run a reaction of fatty acid and chlorosulfonic acid and that makes the base for the detergent. Fred was also in charge of the safety and security of the Plant. One early morning I walked into my office and he said Hector there is a drum of chlorosulfornic acid in the storage dripping on the concrete floor. The acid was eating away the floor and generating a cloud of toxic fumes. The drums had two bung-holes and one was one inch in diameter and the other was three inches bung-holes. Fred went to the room where we kept the safety equipment. Fred and two other chemical operators brought the one piece safety suit. They also brought the gas mask and oxygen tank and a bag of soda powder to neutralize the acid spilled on the concrete floor. They helped me to put the suit on and Fred fitted the gas mask on my face and the oxygen tank with the harness on the back. I grabbed a pipe wrench and went into the room and very carefully tighten the one inch bung. I began walking out of the room because I was running out of oxygen. I was signaling with both hands to remove the gas mask from my face. I was running out of air and getting desperate. Finally the two operators came running and removed the mask and the tank from my back. I asked Fred didn't you check the gauge in the oxygen tank? He answered, yes I did! And I gave him a mean look and walked away.

On Christmas 1979 everyone received a Christmas bonus every year. To my surprise when I arrived home after work that day. I had a Christmas card in my mail box from the owner of the fiber glass company. He sent me a check as bonus and was thanking me for the good performance in Puerto Rico. Shortly thereafter we had a company Christmas party at the Holiday Inn and Ed the plant manger announced his retirement, (he was going to retire after Christmas 1980). Everything was normal during the next year and my picture was in the company magazine published in Saint Paul, Minnesota. They showed me filling the one million barrel of detergent without any rejections. This was the equivalent of fifty five million gallons of detergent. Then Christmas 1980 arrived we had our Christmas party at the same Holiday Inn. Like every year the wife's and husbands were invited. The wife of Fred and the wife of his best friend Bob, the analytical technician did not come to the party. The party was on a Saturday evening Ed announced that the following Monday Fred would be the next plant manager. I said to myself, this is the beginning of disaster and right I was.

After two months of his position as plant manager he called me to his office. I went into his office and he did not bother to call me by my name. All he said was "with your salary I can hire three chemist"! Another thing I want you to know that we have too many blacks and Hispanics operators. Beginning today I will do the interviews and the hiring. I said to him all the operators that have been hired and trained are still working with us. They all have good attendance and no accidents. He said that's all for today! I began to think about what he was going to do next, it was the month of November 1981 and I told my wife that I wanted to take three weeks' vacation and go to Florida; my wife also took three weeks of vacation from her job at Abbot Laboratories. We fixed up the RV and we started our trip to Florida. We stopped and camped out for two days at the pioneer village in Fort Myers. We visited the Shell Factory and my wife purchased gifts for the family and friends. From Fort Myers we drove to Homestead Florida we had a wonderful 3 week vacation. After visiting friends we decided to head back home to Illinois. We stopped in Orlando and camped out inside Disney World area for two days. My wife wanted to be home for Thanksgiving. We took a boat ride in Disney World the second evening my wife started getting cold when the water would splash over us. I had a windbreaker on and gave it to her because she was shivering. We returned to the RV and went to sleep. We got up early the next morning and drove all day stopping at a rest area in Kentucky. We parked with the many recreational vehicles already parked there. In the morning we had breakfast at the rest area restaurant. We left driving for ten hours and arrived home on time for Thanksgiving.

On Monday morning when I returned to work the lock of my

office was changed because my key did not open the door. I went to the production area and talked to the operators. Every one of them was very angry and they were calling names, such as that SOB turkey neck and so on! (They called him turkey neck because his skin around the neck was all red and wrinkled just like a Turkey neck). Fred came in every Monday morning late and with a hangover. This Monday he called me to his office and told me that he was making changes. I was more useful working as a shift supervisor and his buddy Bob (turkey neck) was the new production superintendant. He really began his new position in the wrong direction. He wrote a memo for all production personnel and put it on the bulletin board of the lunch room. The memo read, beginning today, only ten minutes for coffee breaks in the morning thirty minutes for lunch and ten minutes for coffee break in the afternoon. When you work at a chemical plant as an operator you are supplied with all necessary equipment including uniforms and safety toed shoes, you are required to change uniforms everyday and take a shower before going home. He had the audacity to write in the memo, no early showers! I asked Bob to put me on the second shift; he told me that Fred wanted me on the day shift. The operators on the day shift asked me if I was going to enforce the new rules, I replied I do not worry about it because every time you go in the lunch room they are playing cards (Fred and Bob).

Four months passed by and Fred called me again to his office. He told me that he was replacing me with a chemical operator Class A. I was to punch a time card and work as a chemical operator. I paused for a moment and said to him you know we met for the first time at the pharmaceutical company in 1960 and you got fired from that company in 1961 and you blamed me. This is 1982; twenty two years later you think you are getting even with me. I calmly said I will not punch a time card because I am still on a salary. I am going to be the best paid chemical operator in the United States and walked out of his office and stopped to talk to the two secretaries in the front office. They could not believe what this idiot was doing to me. The three girls were afraid of Fred and Bob because they constantly harassed and made indecent gestures to them ("no sexual harassment at the time"). The two secretaries kept communicating with the main office in Saint Paul on a daily basis. I asked them to check for me how early I could retire and to mail the information to my home address. Within two weeks I received all the information necessary. Thru all the years that I worked with the company, I had accumulated three hundred and ten days of vacation and sick time. The company would pay me a maximum of one hundred and twenty days at retirement time. The other remaining days if I did not take them I would lose them. I talked to my wife about my plan to retire early. This was March 1982; my wife told me that her supervisor wanted to transfer her to the second shift. I told my wife tomorrow you give your supervisor a two week notice that you are quitting your job. At first she was reluctant. I told her we have been married thirty two years and never been unemployed in the last thirty four years and I was sure we could afford to retire. I did not tell Fred or Bob about my plans to take early retirement, but I called personnel at Saint Paul and the person that answered knew me for many years. She said; Hector, I am sorry about what is happening with you and Fred. He wanted to lower your salary but the company did not allow him to do so. As the plant manager he can designate you to any position he wants for the benefit of the company. I told the girls in Saint Paul that in February 18, 1984, I would be 54 years young at that time after my birthday I would have 81 points with the company's early retirement plan. Because of my years with the company and age I qualified for early retirement I needed only 80 points. I then scheduled my retirement with the secretary for the first week of March, 1984.

Fred and his buddy Bob began looking for excuses to fire some of the operators that were loyal to me through all the years working with them. Then one day he called two operators to Fred's office, he wanted to fabricate a case against me in order to fire me. He asked the two operators to sign a document as witnesses to something I did wrong against the company. The two operators refused to sign the document.

Fred and Bob started having problems in the production area. They had a full warehouse of rejected materials, some of the operators were calling in sick and my successor the production Superintendant enforced another rule. He put another memo on the bulletin board explaining that if you called in sick you must bring in a doctors certificate or you would not get paid for the day. After four weeks of sick leave I returned to work with my Doctors letter. Fred told Bob to have me rework the rejected materials that were in the warehouse. I was surprised when Bob gave me a helper to assist me with the heavy work; 90 percent of the materials were in the acid side and had to be neutralized. The other 10 percent was too high in PH and had to be lowered with hydrochloric acid. I had to wear a gas mask and let the helper handle the hydrochloric acid; we finished removing all of the rejected material and I took a three week vacation.

My wife and I agreed to trade in the motor home for a bigger and better one, then we went south, looked around for a place for retirement but my wife insisted on staying up north with the grandchildren. We looked at the house trailers in pioneer village in Fort Myers, Florida. We liked the double ones and they were very well furnished. After two weeks in Florida we headed back home for Christmas 1983. When the company Christmas party came around I reluctantly agreed to go because my daughter was going with her husband. After the Christmas party I only had two months before retirement. I still had more than enough days left of sick time. I went to my Doctor and he put me on inhalators for asthma. He also wrote a letter to the company that I could not work with chemicals anymore. On March 4, 1984 I retired at the age of 54.

Not being one to sit idle I started woodworking since it's always been one of my hobbies. I began working by contracting the jobs and I figured the amount of materials and cost. Then I added twenty dollars per hour for labor and 10 percent for errors. After working for a year on my own I saved enough money to sell the motor home and buy a 36 foot house trailer. We sold our house to my daughter Hilda at an affordable price. My wife gave me a Baldwin piano for father's day and also an eight foot pool table. We left everything in the house except my working tools. In November 1985 after spending Thanksgiving with the family, we loaded the truck and trailer and started living the life of being retired.

CHAPTER 5
MAKING EXPERIENCE WORK

My wife has been an excellent seamstress for years and after she quit her job she dedicated herself in making dolls and a lot of craft work. She sold dolls from $35.00 to $100.00 dollars apiece. Some of her Dolls are in Germany, Mexico and Puerto Rico. We took two singer sewing machines with us along with her dry goods material for the dolls. Early Saturday morning we headed south in the house trailer and the truck was 52 feet long. The truck had a four hundred horse and two gas tanks with a capacity of forty-two gallons of regular fuel. We arrived at Fort Myers Florida late afternoon on Monday. We drove 1500 miles and the price of regular gas was $ .29 cents per gallon and used 214 gallons and paid only $62.00 dollars. My truck was giving me 7 miles per gallon when pulling the house trailer. With the price of gas at $2.85 cents, and in the year 2010, It would have cost me $610.00 dollars, if I figured that correctly this is an increase of 500% percent for the last 25 years. We parked in a very nice lot near the swimming pool and recreation hall. We opened the 36 by 8 foot canopy that came with the trailer. We had a folding table with four chairs, propane gas grill and set up a nice patio set. Christmas time came and my wife asked me to take her to downtown Fort Myers. They had very nice stores; especially the groceries stores were very abundant with all kinds of products. We purchased Christmas lights for the trailer and we hung them around the canopy. This was our first Christmas away from home. Every year they had a party at the Pioneer Village Hall. We had food, drinks, music, dance, games and a lot of fun. They gave prizes to the youngest and oldest couple. My wife and I won the youngest couple price. They could not believe that we retired so young. Pioneer Village was a three-hundred acres complex divided into three sections. The first section was for seasonal renters like us, from November to May; then the second section was for overnighters or people that stayed just a few days. The third section was private for permanent homes. You could buy a double or a triple completely furnished trailer homes very spacious, well kept and decorated. My wife always wanted to live up north, so buying one of these homes was out of the question. The owner of the village and I became good friends and after two months of living there I celebrated my birthday on February 18, 1985, I turned the ripe young age of 55 years of experience. The owner (Maki) a very humble person asked me if I wanted to work part time for him. He introduced me to his very young girl friend that worked in the office and took care of his business. I took the job part time for 6 hours a day from 4:00 p.m. to 10:00 p.m. By me accepting this job I would receive free parking for the season, telephone in my trailer and all utilities paid. My duties were answering the phone and registering the new campers and lock the front gate at 10:00 p.m. My wife was making her dolls and craft's and selling everything she made. We kept very busy and the winter season went very fast.

The month of May we hitched the house trailer and headed north. Three days later we took route 120 into Waukegan Illinois. We drove west and in 45 minutes we arrived at Fish Lake (RV) Park. This park was not very spacious and modern like the Pioneer Village in Fort Myers. The sites were narrow and barely long enough for my trailer. After 20 minutes of back and forth I finally aligned the RV in the space. This was 1986 and our oldest grandson was eleven years old. He spent all summer with us, fishing and swimming. I went to visit the plant were I retired from, in the front office were the two secretaries still working there. They were happy to see me and their greeting was a big hug. I continued to keep in contact with the two secretaries after I retired, they said we have good news for you, Fred was fired in a very shameful way, we received a letter from Saint Paul and we posted it on the bulletin board. The letter read you are terminated, you no longer work for this company effective today! Hector, we wish you were here to see his face on Monday morning, we told him to look on the bulletin board. He darted out in a hurry and did not bother to say good bye to anyone. By the way did you receive a letter telling you about the two increases in your pension? I replied yes I did and it came in handy, but I did not know those were the two years that Fred denied me of a raise.

The new manager came to the office and shook my hand. He said I have heard a lot of good things about you, your too young to be retired, would you consider returning back to work for us? I replied, I am not exactly retired, my wife and I are traveling every six months, we keep very active and we are financially stable. He told me that they were going to have a Christmas Party and we would like to invite you and your wife always! All you have to do is to call us two weeks in advance. Your daughter mentioned it to me last Christmas by the way I know your son'-in-law he works the third shift. He is the best operator we have had for the last 3 years, and he is getting the perfect attendance bonus. The new manager went back to his office and the secretaries were ready to go out for lunch, they asked me to join them. During lunch they told me that the engineers and operators met and wrote a letter to the company President in Boston, MA. They all signed the letter and sent it certified mail. They explained in the letter the reason why you took early retirement. They also wrote about the problems they were having in the production area. The two girls were very happy with the new Manager. They said something else that you should know is that Bob is no longer the Production Superintendant. The new manager transferred him back to the analytical lab. Bob and Fred's wives divorced them. Bob was in the Hospital for three days; his wife's younger boy friend broke his nose and blackened his eyes. We finished our lunch and the secretaries would not allow me to pay the bill. I went fishing at Fish Lake, after fishing I called my daughter and told her I would be visiting and picking up some of my books I had left when I sold her the house. My daughters have been giving me books for my birthday and Christmas gifts. Books help understand life better or you can compare with other person's experience.

Was I resentful about what Fred and Bob did to me? Some resentment driven people "clam up" and internalize their anger, while others "blow up" and explode on others because they were the first person that approached after a bad experience. Resentment always hurts more to oneself than the person you resented. While your offender has probably forgotten the offense and goes on with his life, you continue to stew in your pain by perpetuating the past. Those who have hurt you in the past cannot continue to hurt you unless you hold on to the pain through resentment. Your past is past nothing will change the past for you are only hurting yourself with your bitterness. If anything, learn from the past to change the present and future. The Bible states to worry about resentment would be a foolish senseless thing to do.

After spending summer at Fish Lake, the month of November came too soon, with heavy resentment I went back to the plant to say goodbye to my co-workers, and advise the secretaries that we would not be able to attend the Christmas party. The secretary told me that Fred couldn't find a job and went to Wisconsin to live with his son. His son was the only family he had from his first marriage. His son went to work one morning and when he came home he found Fred on the floor dead. He died of a massive heart attack. I replied, I hope the good Lord took him, the Bible says in the book of Proverbs; do not withhold good from those who deserve it, when it is your power to act. Do not accuse a man for no reason when he has done you no harm. The Lord's curse is on the house of the wicked but he blesses the home of the righteous. The wise inherit honor, but fools hold up to shame. I went back to Fish Lake and told my wife what had happened. She made a remark.... The poor guy is gone! We all have our final day and will have to answer to the supreme judge, blessed is he whose transgressions are forgiven, whose sins are covered. Blessed is the man whose sins, the Lord does not count against him and in whose spirit is no deceit.

After living in the house trailer, and traveling every six months from Fish Lake to Fort Myers my wife became tired of that kind of living and asked me to sell the house trailer and the truck, she wanted us to move to Puerto Rico and take care of her mother. She was very sick and losing her memory. We sold the house trailer and truck to the recreational vehicle dealer. I had to take a big loss in order to get rid of them in a hurry. This was 1988; we talked to the manager of the Lincoln mercury dealer a friend for many years. I told him that we were moving to Puerto Rico and wanted to take a new car with us. He sold me a 1988 Mercury Sable for a good price. I requested a temporary permit to drive the car to Miami Port of embarkation. He gave me a two month permit and drove to Miami with my wife and took a taxi from the Port of embarkation to the Miami airport. We were very lucky, we arrived at the airport and there was a flight to Puerto Rico, departing in one hour with Eastern

Airlines. We boarded the plane and arrived in San Juan, Puerto Rico in two hours and thirty minutes. We called my wife's brother, Felix; he only lived 20 minutes from the airport. He immediately arrived and picked us up and took us to my wife's mother's house. Six days later we received a call from the customs officer notifying us that our car had arrived and ready for pick up. He told me that it was going to cost $6000.00 to pay the Commonwealth of Puerto Rico for the excise tax. Felix took me to the customs house in San Juan and the officer working for the Port took me to my car and opened the car trunk and asked, what, do you have in this crate I explained that they were my power tools. Before he started opening the crate I gave him a tip for helping me with the check out process, most people told me I would be there all day and I was out of the Port within an hour. (I ended paying $5000.00 dollars to the commonwealth). I already had the clear title for the car; we paid cash for the Sable. As I was driving out of the port I took the wrong turn and started driving on the lane assigned for public transportation only. Immediately I saw the blinking lights of a patrol vehicle I did not stop and the police officer came along side my car and signaled me to stop. I pulled out of the lane when I saw the big public bus approaching, and then realized that I was heading the wrong way. The officer asked me for my license I only had an Illinois driver's license and the temporary permit. He glanced at my last name and asked, are you related to the Judge of the Supreme Court in San Juan. I replied yes, she is my niece, my sisters-daughter. He told me then her brother Eric the criminalist attorney is your nephew, I replied that's correct. He told me that he knew my father because he was born in the same town I was born. He handed me the driver's license and permit back. I asked him where was the office for registering the vehicle and getting the license plates of Puerto Rico. He smiled and told me where I had to go by the "golden mile". He said follow me I am going that way. The traffic was heavy but we arrived within 15 minutes. He also kept talking about my grandfather, who was the owner of most of the land around this area. I replied, yes I know and they sold the land for peanuts. We parted and I went and paid for my license plate and car registration. Afterward, I drove to the house where I was born, it was very different now. Before, the house I lived in was all wood and smaller. Now it was much bigger and built of concrete. I walked around the area and saw three houses all in one block. All my uncles' houses where my grand-mothers; whom died when I was 12 years old and they were rented and my oldest sister collected the rent. My wife and I started looking for a house and bought one at an early age. We never liked to live in other people's houses', including our own children's. My wife's cousin lived out in the country near the Rain Forrest "El Yunque" in Rio Grande. This area was beautiful with mountains and hills; we went to visit on a Sunday. We arrived and they were playing dominoes and cooking outside in the big Pagoda "outside hut". My wife's cousin had three sons and two daughters, of the 5 children 4 were married and had their own families. The youngest son was challenged in a wheelchair and his parents took care of him. My wife had also nostalgia for her birth home, so I asked if they knew of a property for sale in the area. They said you just came at a right time. Let's go in front of the house and I will show you a property for sale. Their house was down in the valley, he pointed up to the hill and there was a 2 story all concrete beautiful mansion. My wife said lets go see it. We all drove up the hill and had to put my car in second gear to make it up to the house.

The owners were a retired couple who showed us the house and the land. The house was very big and well built. There were about thirty giant rocks all over the two and a half acre property and all kinds of fruit trees. Avocado, bananas, plantains, oranges, grapefruit, and there were 23 types of fruits. The first floor was a brand new apartment. We talked to the owners about the selling price. When they told us the price my wife and I looked at each other, and said since it is Sunday please gives us until Tuesday so we can discuss the price and look at other houses. The couple replied we have heard that story before. People come and look and they never come back. I told the couples do not judge us by other people's character, we are people of integrity. We departed and returned to our cousin's house, as we were driving and laughing because we estimated the house might cost, and we were $60,000.00 dollars off in our favor! Sunday we talked about the selling price of the house and the location and we liked the house. On Monday we decided to make an offer, we returned to the home; again my wife told me that the property is beautiful very private, but it would be too much work for us. Hector I know how you are and you are going to become a slave to this property.

And when you discuss the price make an offer $22,000.00 dollars less than their asking price.

I told my wife to talk to them as I would be embarrassed to do that. I stayed inside the car and Geno went and talked to the lady; she got very angry and refused the offer.

The husband walked to me and said; lets discuss this by the mango tree up on the hill. When we arrived at the hill we sat down under the mango tree. He told me that they were selling the house because they had too, not because they wanted to. We purchased the land and built the house. The original owner of the farm segregated 300 plus acres and some are one and a half acres. This house sits on 1 ½ acres, the lot next to the house also is 1 ½ acres, I have all the surveys of both properties. I hired an architectural engineer to do the plans and obtain the necessary permits and started building the home with plenty of help from members of the church and friends. After one year of hard work we completed the house. At that point I ran out of money and we are living on a fixed income to make ends meet, but then the original owner came and cleaned the lot next to mine and cut down some trees, he walked up the hill towards my house yelling and cursing. You put your house on part of my land! I could not believe what he was saying. We went to his lot and he showed me where the iron rods were driven into the ground to mark the lots boundaries. He was right we built the house ten feet inside his lot. He gave me two choices, either you knock the house down or you buy my lot at a market price. I had no choice and had to take a mortgage on the house to buy his lot. My problem is Mr. Padron; the amount of money my wife and I receive from the Social Security is the minimum. For the last six months we have been paying the interest only on the loan, the principal always stays the same. All the people that come to see the house want to buy it, but when I tell them what I am telling you now, they change their minds and leave. Very sadly and with watery eyes he said I cannot sell the house unless the lot is paid off! I shook his hand and I told the man that I would buy the house along with the lot next to it for the amount you were asking. We walked down the hill back to the house; our wife's were having coffee and chatting very friendly. They had already agreed on a selling price for the house. The problem was that the lady did not tell my wife about the lot next door that comes with the house. My wife told me that she agreed to buy the house. I told my wife the problem and that we would have to buy the lot next to the house also, I will explain it to you on the drive back. I told the couple that I was going to discuss this with my attorney and will call them back. I explained the circumstances of the property to my wife. The next morning we went to the house and picked the couple up and drove to the attorney's office. He wrote a contract with the buyers, (us) paying off the empty lot and we both signed and we would take that contract to the bank holding the mortgage first, and that we would pay cash for the property structure on the day of closing. We took the sellers back to the property and stopped by my wife's cousin's home. They were very happy to know we were buying the property.

Tomorrow morning I told my wife, I will take you to the airport and you go to Chicago and take the deed of the two acres of land we have in Waukegan and sell them. I will go to San Juan and talk to the stock broker and sell the Gillette stocks, the stocks were at the time $120.00 dollars a share, which was the highest the stock market had been in the last 50 years. Two weeks after my wife had left; she called me and said that the city planner wanted to buy the land. I told my wife that he probably wanted the land because the sewer and water was arriving in the area of the lots. I told her to ask for 3 times the amount we paid. The results was he was bothered, and told my wife that we will never be able to do anything with the land, as long as he was the city planner. Unfortunately what this manipulator did not know, was that the Mayor of the city has been elected for the last twenty years by the Hispanic vote! So I instructed my wife to tell the manipulator that I will arrive in a couple of days and that I will talk to the Mayor he is a very good friend of mine. After my wife told the city planner of my intentions, he bought the land at 2 ½ times for the amount we paid!

My wife stayed in Illinois waiting for me to call her for the closing on the land in Puerto Rico so she could fly down. While I was waiting for the closing, the couple called me and told me that they would buy the land back and pay me interest and attorney fees, because they had a couple from New York City, that they had made a better offer for the property. I replied it's too late now, the lady replied your wife did not want to buy the property anyway. I replied, I will call my wife and ask her! I called my wife and she told me with an angry voice tell that lady that we do want the property. I told my wife to come back to Puerto

Rico immediately. I called the attorney and told him we had the money and to set up a closing date. The sellers called me again and I told them to talk to my lawyer. My wife arrived for the closing of the purchase of the property. On the closing day the couple was very quiet, they did not say too much. The contract was signed by both parties and the sellers had 2 weeks to vacate the property.

We did not have any furniture, appliances or dishes. We went and purchased everything we needed and set a date after the property was to be vacated. When we arrived with the truck full of furniture to the home, they were still in the house with all of their belongings. I told them to move their belongings to the apartment downstairs. They were supposed to move them out the next day. The lady was still very angry and was yelling and calling her husband a failure. She was so angry that she had about sixteen beautiful orchid plants and she had agreed to sell them to my wife at a cost of $25.00 dollars per plant. When my wife gave her the money, she said they are now $35.00 dollars each. My wife replied twenty five; (my wife is set in her ways especially when it comes to money!) I had to intervene and told my wife that I would pay the $35.00 dollars. The sellers had two dogs a black German shepherd and a Chihuahua. They came over the next day with church members to pick up their belongings. They asked me if I could keep the dogs because they had no place to keep them. I agreed to keep them and ended up with a house and three dogs. My brother-in-law had given me a one year old bull terrier. This dog was all white with a big head and short stubby legs. He hated cats and little kids. Two weeks after we moved in I told my wife that I needed a pickup truck to work around the land. The grass and bushes were very high and without any power tools I was not able to do the yard work. The only Sears Roebucks store available was two hours away. My wife stayed home because her cousin was coming to help her around the house. Early Monday morning I drove the Mercury Sable 1 ½ miles to the highway which went into San Juan. As I drove to the first town which was Rio Grande, then to Canovanas the next town on highway route 3, I saw a car dealership. At the dealership was a 1987 Ford pickup truck, the truck was a ½ ton with a 237 engine and it looked like new.

I needed a used truck, I parked next to the truck and started looking at it, then a short heavy set man came out of the office, he said hello, he looked at my car and asked did you bring that car from the states? I replied that's right! He said I see you are looking at this pickup; it was brought from Chicago, Illinois. He replied that the Mercury Sable was the first one he had seen in Puerto Rico. They sold the model Taurus because it was $3000.00 dollars cheaper. I asked him how much, are you selling the truck for. He said this truck is like new, and it has very low mileage let me go get the keys so you can test drive. He came back with the keys and asked me my name. I replied, Hector Padron, he almost fainted and he hugged me, "do you know who I am, he said, I replied no, he said I am the chubby boy that you defended at school about forty years ago. I even remember when you fought for the long black haired girl. Seems like every day you got into a fight!

I laughed and told him, I said the long haired girl is my wife now. Then we got in the truck and drove it for twenty minutes and returned back to the office and he showed me the title of the truck and how he acquired the truck. He said that a man from Chicago brought the truck to Puerto Rico for his brother. When his brother went to pick up the truck at the customs house he did not have the money to pay the dues to the commonwealth. My friend bought the truck from the man and paid the dues. He gave me a very good deal and offered to finance the truck for me. I told him that I was paying cash. We made the deal and he drove the truck and I drove my car to my new home. When we got to the house he looked around and said, Hector you have a mansion here. Looks like you have made a very good investment! He made a remark, it's in the blood; your ancestors were land owners! He did not see my wife because she went shopping with her cousin. When my wife and cousin came home from shopping they saw the truck on the driveway.

Geno's cousin said my God your husband doesn't waste any time. My wife replied that man has been that way all of his life. We took the truck out and drove for two hours. My wife really liked it and was happy that I bought it. I then began buying the equipment I needed. This was the month of August 1989, I purchased one electric generator, three five gallon gas tanks, one self propelled lawn mower, two thirty two-cc grass trimmers, two chain saws, one come along, one hundred feet of rope and two machetes. My wife could not understand why I was buying so much. She was to find out soon enough! In September Hurricane Hugo hit and entered thru the east coast of Puerto Rico, right thru the Rain Forest where we were living. I went to the grocery store and bought canned food, candles, matches a propane gas stove with a full cylinder of gas. I filled the three gas containers, the truck and the car. My wife's cousin house was not a concrete house. It was built with lumber and two by fours. The roof was galvanized panels so they stayed with us. Hurricane Hugo was approaching Puerto Rico and was very strong according to the weather forecasters. Winds of 180 miles per hour with torrential rain we called my wife's cousin and told her to bring all the food she had and suit cases with their clothes and important documents. The apartment downstairs was empty and they moved in. I went to the nearby hardware store and they had a truck load of 55 gallon blue plastic drums. I purchased four drums and four five gallon buckets. The best thing we had in the area was the water. The water came from the rain forest (El Yunque) that was at twelve hundred feet above sea level. The water pressure was very high that I had to install a pressure regulator by the water meter. The area we had was farm land with a septic tank. Our house was built like a fortress out of concrete with half inch iron rods. The windows were metal frames with double thick glass panels. The panels were thirty inches horizontal and six inch vertical blinds. We liked them because they were like awnings with a crank to open and close.

The day before Hurricane Hugo hit us, we were going to get plywood panels to cover the windows. I knew that the windows were very strong and secure; I also told my wife that if any of the windows gave up we will go in the laundry room next to the kitchen.

In Puerto Rico normally the day begins at 5:00 a.m. and it does not get dark until 8:00 p.m. The day Hurricane Hugo hit, it started getting dark around 3:30 p. m., I put the car in the drive way (marquesina) on the first level. It was big enough for one car; I put the truck behind it away from the big mahogany tree that was near the driveway. When it got dark my wife and I went to the big porch on the second level. This porch was in the front of the house overlooking the rain forest. The porch has half inch square iron rods protecting the porch. It began to rain very heavy with strong gust of wind. We had to go inside and lock the door. The wind and rain kept increasing in power and it sounded like a herd of angry bulls. We began getting water seeping from underneath the back door. My wife went to the linen closet and got some towels and put them against the bottom of the door, but the water kept sipping in, we kept on picking up the rain water with the towels and squeezing them into the laundry tub nearby. After ten hours of squeezing towels my wife got tired and went to bed. I stayed up and kept going for 17 straight hours. Hurricane Hugo stayed in the area until the next morning 8:00 a. m. then it started moving toward the ocean only ten miles away from the house, then it disappeared in a matter of minutes. My wife got up and we stepped out into the front porch. My God! We said at the same time. We looked down into the Valley and all the homes built with concrete were still there. We could not see the cousin's house. Two hours after the Hurricane began the electricity, telephone and water stopped working. All the trees were down including 14 coconut trees in front of the house. They were down on the road below, piles of avocados, coconuts, bread fruits, etc. The bananas and plantains were all over the ground. The electric poles were down from where we were all the way to San Juan. We went downstairs to check with the cousins and they were fine. I told them that I was afraid there house was gone, we could not drive to their home because my driveway 134 feet long was completely blocked by debris and the street was also blocked. My dogs were cuddled up under the indoor stairway by the marquee. They were very scared and trembling. We walked to the street and the front entrance gate was gone. There was a small car wedged between two tree trunks. We walked to our cousin's house and it was completely gone. The bath tub was there but the toilet was split in two pieces, they had tears in their eyes.

My wife said thank God that you stayed with us. God brought us here for a reason. The three dogs and the four cats they had disappeared and all the kitchen cabinets, furniture, everything was scattered all over. We were without electric power and city water for two months. We went back home and walked around the perimeter of my land there was a lot of debris from the mountains of the rain forest. The rain Forrest and all the vegetation were destroyed. I noticed the telephone line was disconnected from the house outside. A big branch fell on the line and knocked it down. I went down to the street and noticed that the telephone lines were still attached to the poles, I returned to the house to get my extension ladder and connected the line to the box on the wall, went inside, and praise the Lord we had a working line. We were very excited the phone worked and we immediately phoned our daughters. They were relieved to hear from us. I heard my wife tell my daughters your father is a survivor and prepared for everything, we had enough fuel to run the generator for seven days and we had equipment to start cleaning up. Early the next day I started running the generator and four hours later it would turn off automatically. I made sure that the refrigerator freezer was working because we had 12 buckets of ice inside. I left the generator off for 4 hours and turned it back on to run 4 hours. My wife would do the laundry once a week and we put 4 clothe lines in the back yard with the hot sun and nice fresh wind, the clothes would dry in a couple of hours.

Three days after the Hurricane most of the gas stations were operating with generators. We luckily had plenty of rain water and I would drive to the river and get water for the toilet. We had eight empty milk gallons and my wife boiled the water and would add 1 drop of Clorox per gallon. We let the water cool off and checked the P. H. and fill the milk gallons and place the water in the refrigerator. During this whole ordeal we always had drinking water.

The electric company started working in the metropolitan area first, and I hired a worker to help me clear the debris and the fallen trees. We made big piles on top of the hill. The top of the hill was a half acre flat and every day we burned the debris. FEMA came to the area and asked if we needed anything, we replied that we only lost the fruit trees and vegetation. They told me to go to the Agronomy School at the University of Puerto Rico, they were sponsored by the government and they would give us trees, seeds and fertilizer according to the acres owned.

It was two months later before the electricity and water were restored. Our cousins received funds from FEMA and built a beautiful one story concrete house. I called the company that made electrical iron remote gates; they stop by and measured the area to build and sixteen foot long gate with remote control. There was a home owner's association meeting for the area and he asked the community how they could help. Everyone had their requests and when it was my turn, I requested to get rid of the big rocks in my yard. He visited my house and looked around; he suggested the best way to get rid of those big rocks' was to bury them. He said that he knew the director of public works in Rio Grande. Two weeks later early Monday morning I heard my dogs barking, I looked out and there were public works personnel with an excavator and a bulldozer; the operator of the equipment shook my hand and said, Mr. Padron I know your relatives in San Juan. I smiled and shook his hand and didn't want to talk about my family because I had an altercation with an attorney. I was with a friend a school teacher in the area; we were at the race track (Hippodrome) and in the club house while eating a sandwich next to us two guys (both attorneys). They were drinking excessively because of all the empty drinks at their table. I hear one of them say in Spanish that daughter of a prostitute found my client guilty and I know he is innocent when he mentioned my niece name. I replied she is my niece and my sister is not a prostitute. He again repeated the same words. I stood up and said stand up big mouth. What are you going to do? He said you'll soon find out I replied. As soon as he stood up I clobbered him on the jaw and down he went I was watching his friend as he looked at his friend lying on the floor out! Two security men came and shook the hand of the teacher I was with. They asked what happened. The school teacher told them what had happened and they escorted the two lawyers out of the club house. I was wondering why security did not say anything to me. After they escorted the lawyers out, they returned to the table where we were sitting. One of the two security men said, Mr. Padron that guy you just hit is an alcoholic, he had problems here before and we know your sister, niece and your nephew, he is the best criminal lawyer in San Juan. He is also a member of the Nationalist Party like we are. I know he became a member of the party when he was a student at the University of Puerto Rico. My friend the teacher said Hector I already knew you before you moved into your home. Your nephew told me you were buying the property not too far from my house. From your wife's cousin's house you are close enough to walk to my house. After working with the excavator and the bulldozer, we buried all the big rocks.

CHAPTER 6
OBSTACLES' IN LIFE

Christmas 1989 arrived and we had a big party at our cousin's house that lived in the Metropolitan area, everything was back to normal but there were people still waiting for FEMA to approve their claims. Exactly three years after Hurricane Hugo in the same month of September. The second Hurricane hit right thru the same route of the Rain Forrest, devastation and two more months without electricity this is 1992. My wife's parents were starting to show their age (92 and 78, Rafael and Angelina). Angelina was confined to a wheel chair, my wife would drive every day to their house they lived in a two apartment house in the metropolitan area. My wife's brother Gaspar was separated from his wife and was living with them. My other brother-in-law Felix lived with his wife in the upstairs apartment. My wife started getting tired and upset because all the work we had after the Hurricane. I started drinking more than usual, a six pack of beer and a bottle of Vodka every day after I would work around the yard. I turned my back on God and stopped going to Church. I started betting on the horses at the race track. Rafael my father-in-law fell while taking a shower, we took him to the Veterans Administration Hospital and he did not recover, he passed away. He was buried at the National Cemetery in Bayamon, Puerto Rico. Angelina my mother-in-law started losing her memory and she was starting to be violent. The family decided to take her to a Nursing home. After 1 year in the Nursing Home she passed away. She was buried alongside Rafael at the National Cemetery. Gaspar my brother-in-law moved into a one bedroom apartment. Felix moved with his wife to the first floor and rented the upstairs. In1995 the third Hurricane hit in the same month of September. This time it did more damage to the metropolitan area. My discouraged wife told me we have been in Puerto Rico and for six years we have been thru three Hurricanes. I do not want to live in Puerto Rico anymore. I came here to take care of my parents and now I would like for you to sell the property. I told my wife that I would hire a surveyor and segregate the land and my nephew recommended a good surveyor from San Juan. He came and took all the measurements and placed all the stakes on the ground. I asked him how long it takes to do the process and get the new deed. He said I can do my part in six months. Luckily it was completed in one year. I called my niece Haydee, to help me sell the land she replied this weekend. It was noon when she arrived so I had to walk to the gate and when I open the gate I saw a black Porsche. They pulled into the drive way with my sister and her boy friend, a much older man. My niece introduced me to her boy friend and he said that he had heard a lot about me. He said I here you are selling this property; it's a very private and beautiful place. Why are you selling? My wife wants to go back to Illinois she misses the grandchildren. He put his hand on my right shoulder and said tell you what, I would like to buy this property, give me a price and I will buy it. I thought he was joking or kidding around. I did not answer him, and he said come on uncle try me. I am paying you cash under one condition. What's that I replied, I will write a note saying that the property belongs to me and you and your wife sign it? You keep the deed to the property in your name. I told him that I was going to think about it. Before they left, my sister said to me, I have a two bedroom apartment by the beach ten minute drive from here. We spent weekends and vacations there. You and Geno are welcome any time to stay there. I knew my sister was traveling very often, more than normal. My sister and niece were going to Italy, France, Spain, Germany and time square in New York City. I told my wife, something is very strange and not right about my niece's boy friend. I am not going to sell him this property.

My wife wanted to visit the grandkids in Illinois so I took her to the airport and bought a one way ticket to Chicago, and then she told me I don't know how long I am going to stay there. I replied okay whatever you wish, and then I stayed home all alone with the dogs.

One month later I received a call from Justin, my grandson. He was calling from Cook County Hospital in Chicago, I left for Chicago immediately! Justin's dad had a stroke so immediately I called American Airlines and they told me that the only way I could get to Chicago in the next eight hours was to fly to North Carolina and then to Chicago. Although it was much more costly to find I had to take that flight. I arrived in Chicago at one in the morning and Justin was waiting for me. On the way to the Hospital he explained what happened, my grandson has been playing basketball since he was in grade school. Now he was playing in college and doing very well. His father (Don) never missed any of Justin's games. That Friday night they were playing for the semifinals. My son-in-law Don, for many years was taking aspirins for headaches and never bothered to see a doctor. That day he was not feeling well and went to the game with his son and let his son drive. They arrived at the gymnasium and the game started shortly after. Justin noticed that his father sat way in the back on the last bench he would always sit right close to the team bench. Ten minutes into the game Justin looked up and saw his father slumped on his right side. He ran up the bleachers to his father tried to help him but there wasn't any response. Thank God, the hospital was right across the street! They rushed him into the emergency room; they found that his heart and vital organs were functioning. The problem was that the right side of his brain was completely blood clotted. The surgeon operated him immediately and opened his skull from the forehead to the back of his head. They removed all the blood from the brain and in the process; part of his brain was scraped.

When I arrived at the hospital, there were relatives, pastors, and members of different Churches present. They were all praying for the Lord to spare his life. No one was permitted to see him at the moment. My daughter Abby and I went to the nurse in charge and asked if we could see him, she replied no sir, the doctors order's are that we will have to wait 24 hours, my daughter and I insisted to see him and she allowed us to see Don for a short moment. There he was all wired up to various machines to keep his organs functioning. He was completely brain dead and his body cold. I told Abby lets all go home and come back tonight. It was already 4:00 a.m. My grand-children were devastated and inconsolable. They were very, attached to their father and had no hope that he was going to survive we went home and rested for a few hours and returned to the hospital it was a one hour drive from the house. The doctor at the hospital told us that if her husband did not wake up in the next three days, they will have to disconnect all the machines. The three days passed and Don's mother, brothers and sisters were at the hospital when we arrived. We had a meeting in the waiting room. My daughter said a beautiful prayer and asked God to do his will. One by one my daughter asked his relatives for their opinion, if he should be disconnected and let him go in peace. The doctor already had told them if he didn't wake up he would be in a permanent coma. Don's mother said that she did not want her son to live that way, and my daughter turned to me and asked me what do you thing? I replied; it is too early we should wait at least seven days. My daughter talked to the doctor and told him that we were going to wait. He looked upset and asked my daughter, do you want to donate his organs. My daughter almost fainted. My Daughter told the doctor <u>you do your job and my God will do his</u>! He took us to the room where Don was located. The doctor replied watch this, he grabbed Don's belly and squeezed it with both hands and left his fingers marked on his belly and said you see he has no feelings. The doctor left the room. Abby stayed praying to her God to save her husband.

My daughter and I were the only ones going to the hospital every day and then on the seventh day we went late in the afternoon on the way to the hospital my daughter told me, that Audrey her cousin called her and said she had a vision, that I was standing on a rock praying and looking down on my husband. She said that I shouted three times the name of Jesus wake up, wake up, wake up.

When we arrived at the hospital and the doctor was in the room. He said to my daughter, I want you to understand that if your husband comes out of his coma, he is not going to be the same person he was before his stroke. My daughter replied to the doctor I trust my God and I will accept my husband the way the Lord returns him to me! I was getting upset and restless with the doctor's and my daughter noticed. The doctor looked at me and said I just want your daughter to understand. She is a young beautiful woman and if her husband comes out of this he could be a vegetable, aggressive or violent, he finally gave up and left the room. It was seven in the evening and my daughter said I do not have a rock to stand on and there was a stool in the room and I placed it close to the bed and told the nurse that we were closing the door to pray and did not want to be disturbed. My daughter climbed on the stool and began praying looking at the body and speaking in different languages. She only prayed for less than one minute and at the end of the prayer she shouted in English, Don in the name of Jesus wake up, she repeated it three times. His body shook like if he wanted to get out of the bed. I yelled praise the Lord Alleluia!! My daughter got off the stool and looked confused and I asked her if she saw when her husband shook violently on the bed, she replied no! She was very quiet and wanted to go home on the way home she said Dad I think we should go to bed early tonight. Tomorrow will be the eighth day since he had the stroke, then we went home. We must get up early, talk with the doctor, and let God do his will! We went to bed early and I told my wife what happened at the hospital. Exactly at six in the morning the telephone rang. My daughter answered it. It was the doctor calling from the hospital. Your God did his work he said, your husband woke up this morning! We got all excited, dressed and forgot to eat breakfast. We drove to the hospital and arrived before eight in the morning. As my daughter and I were walking down the hallway a housekeeper asked me are you the father of the miracle man? I said I am the father-in-law. We arrived to the room and there he was no machines or wires hook up. I was surprised because we stood in front of him and he said "pop", when did you come in? I said Eight days ago. Don returned home and he was put on medication. He had to take physical therapy at home. His right arm and hand were numb and his speech was slurred Contrary to the doctor at the hospital he turned out to be a humble person.

The summer of 1996, my oldest daughter Hilda sent my sixteen year old grandson (Charlie) to spend the summer with us. He was six foot two inches tall already. He liked Puerto Rico and was surprised when he saw the bananas, mangos, coconuts and all the fruits we had on our land. The first morning he got up early and fixed his own breakfast. He dressed with working clothes and he said grandpa I am ready to help you work on the farm. I said after I have breakfast! We went up the hill and showed him how to use the tools. We had snakes and iguanas and on hot days they climbed up the trees to cool off. One day a big iguana about thirty inches long not including the tail, jumped down from the tree and ran very fast across the yard, my grandson did not know what it was; and replied grandpa is that the "Chupacabra"! Chupacabra is the animal that sucks out the blood of animals but no one has seen it. I started laughing and told him that the iguanas and the black snakes were harmless. Then we went for a ride to Luquillo Beach, where there were many little stores named Kiosk. He was very excited when he saw the beach. We even stopped at one of the Kiosk and we played billiards. Charlie wanted something to eat I offered him some money and he told me I have money grandpa! (Charlie was very mature and very responsible since he was 9 years old). He went walking around the other Kiosk there were more than 27 Kiosk. He came back and I was watching him talking to the lady behind the counter he came back with a big tray of food and a bottle of beer. I asked him did that lady understand you. Charlie replied yes she understood very well she does not speak English and I spoke to her in Spanish. I began to laugh and he asked what so funny grandpa? You do not speak Spanish, Charlie said yes I do mom has been teaching me. I said excellent it is good to be bi-lingual. Later when we arrived home, I told Charlie that tomorrow we are not going to work, because I am calling my sister and ask her for her apartment keys, since the apartment is right on the Ocean front.

When I called my sister she was very happy and eager to meet my grandson for the first time. She told me that it would be the best time because it was Friday and everyone comes for the weekend. There were four buildings with six apartments in each building. My sister's apartment was on the second floor. Early Saturday morning we went to Luquillo beach but my wife was going to visit her brothers Felix and Gaspar in the Metropolitan area. So Charlie and I jumped into the pickup truck and in fifteen minutes we arrived at the apartment. People in PR know how to party especially during the Holidays. When we arrived my sister opened the electric gate and directed us to a parking space. This was a very private place surrounded with an 8 foot fence. We spent the day with my sister playing dominoes and swimming at the beach. Charlie had a wonderful time and fell in love with Puerto Rico. Summer passed; One week before his departure, he talked to his grandma. He wanted to stay with us and go to school in Puerto Rico. We told him that he could stay and attend a bilingual private school, so he called his mother and she told him that he had to come back home. He was very sad and told us that as soon as he turned eighteen he was coming to live with us.

After Charlie left, Gaspar had to be taken to the VA Hospital. He had diabetes and was drinking heavily and not eating properly. He had a bad infection on his left foot and it kept eating away and would not heal. They finally amputated his left foot. The infection kept progressing and became gangrene. They had to amputate his left leg at the knee. Every Sunday we would visit him at the VA Hospital and take him chicken soup. As soon as he ate his soup, he would ask me to sing a gospel song. His favorites were "The Rugged Cross", "In the Garden" and "What a Friend We Have in Jesus". One Sunday we went to the hospital earlier than usual and he was not in his room, we asked the nurse and told us that he was in the recovery room. We went to see him and there he was lying down. His right leg was amputated at the knee. My wife started crying and I had to take her out of the room. One thing that amazed me about Gaspar was that he never complained, he always had a smile and told jokes to his sister. This is 1987 and my wife went to visit the family in Illinois. When she arrived there she found out that we were going to become great grandparents. My daughter Abby's son Justin while in college got his girl friend pregnant. The baby boy was born and my wife had an excuse to stay in Illinois and take care of the baby. I kept on drinking and playing the horses 3 days a week. My wife's second cousin was always checking on me every day. Six months passed by and my wife decided to come home to Puerto Rico. Her brother Gaspar died and was buried at the National Cemetery September 19, 1998 exactly 3 years after the last Hurricane. This was the fourth Hurricane for us but not as bad as the last three. After the Hurricane we had more work again and my wife was tired and wanted to sell as soon as possible and move back to Illinois. Finally a young couple came from New York looking for acreage to buy and I showed them the land that was segregated and two months later they bought it and paid cash for the segregated lot. We made a good profit and my wife was very happy.

CHAPTER 7
AWAKENING BY THE LORD

One Monday morning earlier than usual I had a bench under an Almond tree. This tree was way up on the hill and had survived all four Hurricanes. It was big and strong as I sat down on the bench and lowered my head. I was not praying but I was thinking of a song I use to sing at church in the early part of 1955. My three children were two, three and four years old. The title of the song is "Peace in the Valley" and it went like this.

"I am tired and so weary but I must go along till the Lord comes and calls me, calls me away! When the morning is bright, and the lamb is alive, and the day is dark; dark as the sea there will be peace in the valley for me, some day; there will be peace in the Valley. Oh Lord, I pray! When the bear will be gentle and the wolf will be tame, and the lion will lay down by the lamb, and beast from the wild will be led by a little child, and I will change from this creature that I am, yes Lord".

I heard a flock of birds, many of them, they were flying in a circle above my head for a moment I thought they were going to attack me. It was like in a dream, I felt dizzy. I saw a flash of light very bright and had to close my eyes, I heard God's voice inside my heart. He was saying to me, "I gave you enough time to redeem yourself, you turned your back on me but I have been with you all this time. This is your last opportunity! You are going back to the church, you were born the second time. You are to buy the airfare for you and your wife". All of a sudden I saw the month of May printed in front of me. The house will be sold before your departure. When you get back to Illinois, there is going to be a wooded lot near your daughter's house. You are going to build your house in that lot. I looked up to the sky and I felt a sense of happiness and I prayed, God is omnipotent and mighty we cannot deny it. He is a God of miracles and is written all over the sky. I began singing with a new voice. I Believe, I believe for every Drop of rain that falls, a flower grows, I believe, somewhere in the darkest night a candle glows, I believe for everyone who goes astray. Someone will come to show the way I believe that someone in the great somewhere, hears every word every time I hear a new born baby cry or touch a leaf or see the sky, then I know why! I believe!!

I walked down the hill to the house and my wife had been watching me all the time. She said please stop drinking you are killing yourself on this property. I want you to sell and go back to Illinois with the family. I told her that that is exactly what God wants me to do. She said I saw you up there looking at the sky and a flock of birds flying in a circle. I am glad you saw it; I replied it was the month of January 1999 four months after the last Hurricane had passed. We had four more months before the month of May. I put a sign at the entrance on the electric gate and at the K-mart bulletin board with pictures of the property. Within twenty four hours we started getting calls in regards to the property. The first potential client was a middle aged woman and made an offer. The offer was fifty thousand under the market value my wife was so desperate to sell that she told me to sell it to the lady. I replied no way, we have plenty of time before the month of May. In the month of March a retired couple members of the Pentecostal Church visited and told us that they wanted to buy the property at the price we were selling the house. The only problem was they wanted to sell their house first. A young couple was building a house in the same area. He worked at the Conquistador Hotel as a head waiter. He told me that the leader of the band playing at the Hotel was looking for a house like mine. He came with his girlfriend, a high school teacher. They looked around very carefully and liked the apartment downstairs. The girl friend told the musician that the apartment was ideal for a recording studio. They wanted to buy the property as soon as possible. They agreed to the purchase price that we were asking also the sellers to pay closing and attorney fees. I called my attorney and he suggested calling the buyers and having them bring a registered check for twenty thousand dollars. We went to the attorney's office to sign the contract. The buyers were to secure a first mortgage thru the bank. In any case that the buyers change their mind, the twenty thousand dollars would be forfeited. We signed the contract the first week of March 1999 and the closing to be on the first week of May of the same year. I started making arrangements for moving back to Illinois. We made reservations with American Airlines for Monday two days after closing the sale of the house. I called the moving company and arranged for pick up of our belongings on Saturday the day after the closing. My wife was telling me that I was acting too fast. She has been a very slow person when making decisions. Two men came from the bank to appraise the property. They told my wife that the property was beautiful and it was worth more than what we were selling it for. They said that there was no problem for the bank to approve the loan for the buyers. Three weeks before the closing the buyers got into a fight and broke off the relationship. They terminated the relationship because she found out that he had an affair with one of the women dancers from the band. He called my attorney and wanted the twenty thousand dollars back. The attorney told him that the money was spent already. He also told him that the bank had everything approved and all set for the closing. Again my wife was losing faith and wanted me to call the moving company and the airlines to cancel everything. I told her, I turned my back on God once, and I will never do that again, I am doing what the Lord told me to do you are welcome to come to the bedroom and pray with me. She did not follow me to the room; I knelt down on my knees and started praying. Lord God almighty here I am before you. You knew me even before I was born and you are my creator and were in my care even before I was born, and took care of me from my mother's womb. You did not let me die but gave me life, today that I am old with gray hair and you still take care of me. Lord no matter what the outcome will be, your will be done and I will be faithful to you with body and soul, "Amen" The Bible in the book of Romans 12.13, reads the only accurate way to understand ourselves is be what God is and what he does for us. I started singing one of my favorite songs like I always do after praying.

"I am only human, I am just a man, help me believe on what I could be and all that I am, show me the stairway I have to climb. Lord for my sake; teach me to take one day at a time, one day at a time, "Lord" that's all I am asking from you. Lead me, tell me what I must do, yesterdays is gone and tomorrow may not come, help me today and show me the way," one day at a time", Thank you Jesus!" I walked out of the room and I felt the "Holy Spirit", my wife was smiling and seemed very happy; she hugged me by the waist. I am twelve inches taller than her. Friday on the closing day of the sale, it didn't happen. The moving company was coming to pick up the furniture the next day, Saturday. We had to be at the airport on Monday by noontime to catch our flight. My wife wanted me to cancel the moving and the flight. I told her I have faith and trust God, whatever happens will be God's will. We went to bed early that Friday and the telephone rang at eight in the morning. It was from the bank, the person on the phone asked me, please come down to the bank by nine O'clock this morning. We are doing the closing on your property. This will be the first time in bank history that we do a closing on Saturday. The buyers reconciled and decided to buy the property. My wife and I dress, and we were ready to go in 10 minutes, we hurried to the bank, we were there before nine o'clock. We were out of the bank by ten thirty and the buyers came to the house with us. When we arrived at the house the moving trailer was already waiting. The buyers decided to buy the car and a gas station owner bought the pickup truck. My wife could not believe what was happening. But she was very happy and silent. I quoted some verses from the Bible and told my wife you know I really believe that spiritually speaking. Your mind is your most vulnerable organ. God allows things to happen for us to learn to be positive and trust him. The Bible tells us to keep our minds focused and to fill your mind with good and positive thoughts! In the book of Habakkuk, the Bible reads, these things that are planned would not happen right away but be positive, and slowly, steadily, surely the time approaches when the vision will be fulfilled. It seems slow do not despair for these things will surly come to pass. Just be patient and they will not be overdue a single day. Just remember that a delay is not a denial from God! After the trailer pulled out of the driveway with our household belongings we turned the house keys over to the new owners. They took us to my brother-in-law who lived 15 minutes from the from San Juan International airport. We stayed Saturday and Sunday, and on Monday afternoon we took off and we arrived in Chicago late afternoon. Our youngest daughter and her husband, the miracle man (Don) gave us shelter in his home. Three days after we arrived I went to the Ford dealer and purchased a new pickup truck. On the first Sunday in Illinois, I woke early and began driving toward Waukegan. I wanted to go to the church where I was baptized. All of a sudden I went into a trance, I felt like a magnetic force was driving my truck. I kept driving north and when I realized I had driven to the Wisconsin state line, we were lost! I pulled to the side of the road and began praying and asking God for his guidance, I opened the Bible and read in the book of Daniel and James. "God keeps his promise, and will not allow you to be tested beyond your power to remain firm at the time you are tested, God will give you the strength to endure, and provide you with a way out. "My sense came back to me and I turned around." I headed back south to Waukegan. I was on the road for four hours since I left my daughters house and arrived at the church after the morning service had finished and as I entered the church we saw this lady with a big smile and long white hair. She was alone standing by the entrance. I told her my name and what had happened to me she said you are in the right place. "Welcome", we have been waiting for you, the Spanish service was about to begin at twelve thirty and I started to meet some of the brothers and sisters of the congregation. After the service they had sandwiches and refreshments and stayed for a while and told my brothers and sisters that I was singing the gospel again for the Lord. I never told my wife and daughters that I got lost that morning on my way to Church. The second week after arriving we were with our daughter Abby, my wife and I wanted to look for an apartment to rent within the area. This is still the month of May and the miracle man Don would go for a bicycle ride as my wife and I were stepping out of the house, then Don came running all excited. Pop he said there is a man putting up a sign in a big wooded lot. Let's walk over there and take a look. The lot was on the next street from my daughter's house. I read the for sale sign, the name and telephone number on the sign reminded me, my God, this is my friend that built the house in the year 1969 the house that I bought from his son and then I sold it to my daughter. This man was a very well respected builder and owned a large company that built many apartment complexes. He was born in a farm in Wisconsin owned by his German parents. He was very humble and a good friend. I called him and said this is Hector Padron calling regarding the lot you are selling. You old son of a gun, where are you? He asked, I said I am in Gurnee by my daughter's house; I removed the sign from the lot. He replied I just put that sign up five minutes ago. I said that is my lot. He replied what are you talking about? I owned that lot for thirty five years! I answered I am just kidding I am going over to your house with my wife and we are bringing our check book. He lived fifteen minutes away and arrived to his house within twenty minutes. He always called me "Son of a Gun", there you are he said young and good looking. Are you still singing? I replied yes, singing for the Lord! We talked about the twelve years we were in Puerto Rico and the four Hurricanes we endured. Okay my old friend I said, how much are you asking for the lot. For you no price, what do you mean? I am going to show you and your wife something. He pulled out a picture from a magazine and the blue prints. Look at this house Hector, Four thousand square feet. The lot is three quarters of an acre in a corner of a dead end street. I said I know the area, my daughter lives there for the last fifteen years. We talked it over and we agreed to build the house in four stages. I was to get credit for my labor, so my wife and I decided to stay with our daughter because it would be easy to see the house being constructed instead of having to drive back and forth. We started breaking ground in the month of June 1999. My wife and I began going to Church every Sunday since I accepted Jesus as my savior. I attended Bible studies on Wednesdays evening, one of the Wednesdays we were studying the book of Isaiah. We started reading Chapter 45. I was chosen to read the first four verses. When I read the second verse I stopped reading, the pastor asked me, what is wrong brother? I answered, I have a testimony; the Lord says I am your creator; you were in my care even before you were born. I told the group the experience I had in Puerto Rico, how God talked to me and gave me in detail everything I was to do. He gave me another opportunity to redeem myself. For forty years I was running from regrets and hiding my shame. I was being manipulated by bad memories and letting my childhood experience in controlling my life. I made a lot of mistakes raising my children but I was a provider and the man of the house. I took my anger and resentment out on my family and would explode without any reason. While studying the word of God, I finally realized that those who have hurt me in the past cannot hurt me anymore, unless I hold the pain through resentment. The Bible says; to worry about resentment would be a foolish senseless thing to do.

Romans 12:3 read, "the only accurate way to understand ourselves is by what God is and what he does for us" My youngest daughter gave me a book for Christmas; it was explaining how to pray every day". The book has a poem written by Russell Kelfer and it was so inspiring to me that I memorized it. It goes like this; "You are who you are for a reason, you're part of an intricate plan, and you are a precious and perfect unique design, called God's special man or woman. You look like you look for a reason, Our God made no mistake, he knit you together within the womb, you are just what he wanted to make, the parents you had were the ones he chose and no matter how you may feel, we were custom-design with God's plan in mind and they bear the master's seal, no, that trauma you faced was not easy and God wept that it hurt you so, but it was allowed to shape your heart so into his likeness you grow. You are who you are for a reason, you have been formed by the master's rod, and you are who you are beloved, because there is a God" We worked on the house all summer and I told my friend the builder that I wanted ten inch walls and four inches concrete floors for the foundation. He asked why, and I replied you never know; maybe my great grandchildren want to build a house. By that time the land could be scarce, so they can build on top of this house and the air space is free. You son of a gun he said, no wonder your wife thinks you are crazy. I know my wife thinks that I am crazy and she would say that around the children and they reflected on crazy! Every time the children misbehaved, she would tell them wait until your father gets home, you know how mean and crazy he is, instead of her disciplining them! What my wife didn't know is that I was put on earth to prepare myself for eternal life and not to be remembered; the bible says; remember each of us will stand personally before the judgment of God. Salvation is an individual matter it does not happen in groups. God won't ask you if you are Catholic, Baptist, Pentecostal or any other religion. Deep in my heart I believe that God the father of the universe will have two questions for all of us. In the Bible we can determine that God will have those two questions for us to answer, "First what did you do with my son Jesus Christ?" and the "second question; what did you do with what I gave you?" The first question will determine where you are going to be spending eternity. The second question will determine what are going to be doing in eternity; if you are reading the Bible. I suggest you prepare yourself to answer the two questions!! Going back to the construction of the house, we as humans are imperfect; we violate the Ten Commandments every day. One early Monday morning I walked to the building site as usual. The siding installers were working on the back of the house. It was already the month of March 2000, they had the back wall almost completed and I noticed that they were not installing the vapor barrier before the siding. I told them about it and the foreman said; that's not necessary, I replied for you are not but for me it is, I am the one paying the heating bill in the winter and the air-conditioning in the summer. I called my friend the builder, because he was the one that hired them. He said; Hector I had my son yesterday bring the sixteen feet rolls of plastic, they are in the garage. He came over to the house and told the installers to take all the siding down and start all over again. One of the Ten Commandments reads; "you shall not steal" very seldom I eat at fast food restaurants, like Mac Donald's or Burger King. I take more than one straw for my drink, and only need one, and then put the rest in my shirt pocket, "That is stealing" Sometimes I take a whole bunch of napkins and take them home, "That is stealing" We finished the house in the month of April and moved in the month of May. I did the landscaping all summer of 2000. In the summer of 2001 I built a 16 x 24 foot deck, in 2002 I built a six foot fence around the perimeter of the lot. In 2003 I finished the basement and added another bedroom and full bathroom. We had everything set up to our liking, except there was something missing. My wife said we have plenty of space outside for a tool shed. We went to Home Depot and they had a 10 x 12 foot wood shed. They were selling the kit for three thousand two hundred fifty dollars. My wife said I'll buy it and you put it together. I told her forget it, I will buy the materials and build it myself. We bought the material and built the shed in 8 working days, it was stronger and better built than the Home Depot shed. I spent only twelve hundred dollars, and saved two thousand fifty dollars I have been criticized by ministers and members of the church. If you read this book, you can see from the beginning all my life I have been working. Each project and every investment has been fruitful. On Wednesday evening during the Bible study class. I was asked to read in the book of Matthew 6:19-24, the Bible reads: "Do not store up for your selves, treasures on earth, where moth and rust destroy and where thieves break in and steal. But store up for yourselves treasure in heaven, where moth and rust do not destroy and where thieves do not break in and steal. For where your treasure is, there your heart will be. The eye is the lamp of the body, if your eyes are good, your whole body will be full of light. But if your eyes are bad, your whole body will be full of darkness, how great is that darkness? No one can serve two masters. Either, he will hate the one and love the other, or he will be devoted to one and despise the other. You cannot serve both God and money. After I finished reading the scriptures; one brother said you see brother all the years of hard work and saving money! When you die your son-in-law will inherit everything. I went home that Wednesday night. I was not angry or sad, but my mind was telling me you have a lot of praying to do. I went to the bathroom and sat down on the commode, lowered my head and covered my face with both hands. Tears began flowing from my eyes. I prayed Lord you know my heart; I never intended to get rich or pile up treasures here on earth. You gave me the tools to work with and you planned everything for me when I was in my mother's womb. If I am wrong in my heart to love material things, please take everything away from me. Through the years I have made a lot of furniture for my home, church and other people. I have a book shelve with plenty of books; the majority of the books are gifts. During breakfast I was very quiet and told my wife I am going to relax today. She said you need to rest you look tired. We have a very spacious den (a study room) so I retrieved the first book I saw was a book which was the first book given to me by my daughter. Here is what she wrote in the front of the book:

February 18th 2002, Happy Birthday Daddy! I love you, your daughter Abby: Then she wrote: Psalm 33; sing to him a new song; play skillfully, and shout for joy. For the word of the Lord is right and true; He is faithful in all he does. The Lord loves righteousness and justice; the earth is full of his unfailing love. "Amen" The book titled was the Prayer of Jabez by Bruce Wilkinson, and Jabez called on the God of Israel saying on that you bless me indeed, and enlarge my territory that your hand would be with me; and that you would keep me from evil; that I may not cause pain: God granted him what he requested". There is a misconception about Christian humble people, when I was around thirty two years old. I visited a church that I really liked; I was very well dressed with a suit and tie. I really like to worship with music, singing and clapping my hands. It makes one feel alive and happy, after listening to the pastor's sermon. I was under the impression that God put us on earth to be poor and needy, like in the Old Testament. "I cannot possibly agree with that! Because Jesus said; open your eyes and look at the fields Jesus pleaded they are ripe for harvest." God wants to begin with you now. He is not waiting for you to become someone else before he can use you. He is not waiting for you to go somewhere else. When God sent me back from Puerto Rico to Illinois I did everything he told me to do, he gave me passion, interest, opportunities and capabilities.

CHAPTER 8
CONTINUOUS PRAYER

"In the year 2000 I started praying more than ever, and talked to the Father the son and the Holy Spirit". You do not have to open your mouth, if you have the Holy Spirit "within you". You can talk to the Father twenty four hours a day. I was asking God "please talk to me". This time he talked to me the same way he did in Puerto Rico. I was sitting down on a bench under a crab apple tree in front of the house looking at a cross that I had made out of a pine tree. This cross is sixteen feet tall and overlooks the highway. When I am outside working on the yard, I sit on the bench and meditate looking at the cross. In September 2009 the Lord said to me, "you are going into exile for one year. You are to write a book beginning from your mother's womb"! It was not my first experience with God, so I was very relaxed and calm. On Sunday my wife and I went to church. I went to the front of the congregation and announced that I was going away for one year. I told them that I did not know where I was going but please pray for me. I sang the song "one day at a time" and will never forget that day, September 6th 2009. I never told my wife when I was moving because I did not know. Early Monday morning September 11th 2009, I went for a drive and headed north, before I entered Wisconsin at the Illinois state line. I saw a four story building with sign on the front that read for senior citizens assisted living. I went inside and a young woman greeted me and showed me the premises.

It was not what God wanted for me so I turned back and began driving south on Highway 41 where I had the Pine Cross, seven miles away from my home. These apartment complex buildings had some open apartments for rent, I entered the business office and was given an application I filled it out and the lady at the desk reviewed the application. She then gave me the keys for three apartments to look at them. I moved in September 2009 and decided for the one overlooking the highway on the third floor, very spacious with a sliding door to the front porch balcony. I sit on the recliner and observe the many cars going north from 2:00 p.m. to 7:00 p.m. That tells me that there are many people living in Illinois that work in Wisconsin. To move into the apartment a brother from church Eli, and Don my son-in-law (miracle man) helped me move in. I could not use my right hand for a year because I took a bad fall at home. I dislocated my right shoulder and the pain was horrible. My wife called an ambulance and they took me to the hospital. They put it back and my grandson Justin picked me up from the hospital. When I returned home I went to bed and in the morning I dislocated the shoulder again and back to the hospital and the doctor prescribed pain killers for two months. The fall affected and damaged all the nerves on my right arm and could not close the hand for a year. The first night at the apartment when I started praying before retiring for the night my prayer was Lord God how am I going to write when I cannot close my hand and I am right handed. The Lord wanted me to do a manuscript like in the old times. I went to bed and for many years I get up at 4:00 a.m. to use the bathroom. By instinct I used my right hand and my right hand felt different I used it without any problem, I even made a fist without pain, I started praising God, my hand was healed and able to write. At 4:00 a.m. I could hear my sister Aida's voice saying goodbye to me. I waited until 8:00 a.m. and called her house in Puerto Rico. My nephew answered and I asked to talk with Aida my sister. He paused for a moment and said; mom left us this morning at 4:00 a.m., she was in a coma for five days. I mentioned to my nephew that she came to me in this morning about that same time and she said goodbye! I called my wife about my sister because my sister and her husband were the maid of honor and the best man of our wedding. The last time I talked to my sister she told me that she was prepared to meet the Lord; She talked about our childhood and upbringing when she was 17 and I was 12 years of age and she remembered how I would throw rocks at the boys trying to protect my 3 sisters. I believe she knew her time was near to go meet our maker. The Bible reads in Ecclesiastes 3:1; there is time for every matter under heaven (the Earth) a time to be born and a time to die; a time to plant and time to pluck up what is planted. "Praise is to God".

If you call yourself a Christian and you do not study the Bible, you are wasting your time. I wasted forty years reading the Bible, you can read the Bible but it is not the same as studying the Bible. Christians, congregations, have group Bible study. The purpose is to pray and ask the Father, the son and the Holy Spirit for guidance, wisdom and understanding. February 17, 2010 one day before my 80th birthday, praying Lord God almighty, show me all parts of my life where I still need to change to see the truth you are showing me. The Bible in the book of John 8:12 reads as follows: "I am the light of the world, he who follows me shall not walk in darkness, but have the light of life". God wants us to depart from temptations and he wants us to pray daily for protection from it! God will provide the way of escape for every temptation that you will ever face, you can avoid a lot of temptation by meeting the underlying needs those sin represent in God's honoring ways. The Holy Spirit is ready to give you the comfort you need so you will not feel the need to sin at that moment. The devil will flee from you if you resist him in Gods power. I wish I could turn the hands of time and return to my 40's. I know I would have been a much better husband and father. Satan is on earth and he is very shrewd. Sometimes he uses your own family to make you sin, for many years I have been a victim of circumstances and a victim of love. I am not trying to justify myself, but it is reality and I am a sinner. My wife and oldest daughter Hilda cannot let go of the past. Today is Thursday February 18th 2010 and it is my 80th birthday and still my family brings back the past... I moved into this apartment five months ago and will be surprised if they call to wish me a happy birthday! For many years I have been the villain and my family has admitted that they are part of the problem. No matter what the subject of the conversations, it always ends about the past. God knows that my intentions were with love but perhaps the path I took was the wrong approach. I look back on the past and understand that I made a lot of mistakes raising my children. I was young and now I am old, with better understanding of the damages and trauma I experienced from my childhood and not from my wife and children. Over the time our memories become our identity. Giving up our version of the past, before moving to the apartment my thoughts were who am I? Who are they? I wanted to be the king of my castle but I was not permitted and I started feeling like a stranger in my own home. I have learned during the last five months in exile to remember the good times I have had with my family, going on trips, picnics, swimming, vacation and outdoor memories. You can use the past to observe the person you are today! Remembering the good times we have had together. This time in this apartment has made me understand that there have been more good times than bad and has helped me to love my family even more. If my family would do the same they would see that there are more positive memories than negative. The only way we can reach that positive scale is by understanding that the past is gone and lets' move towards the future. I discovered compassion for myself for the first time, and regret my actions during my 59 years of marriage. I have asked my wife for forgiveness a thousand times and she does not forgive or forget. Compassion allows me to stop outside the emotional field of the bad events and explore the reality of the heavenly forces around my compassion allows me to accept who I am today. Compassion is the way to begin healing the hurting past! For my wife the word compassion and forgiveness do not fit in the same sentence! The good lies underneath the grief, sadness, anger, betrayal and the smoldering resentment of past conflicts. Our family comes from not just the sweet moments remembered, but also from the survival of our struggles. We are not perfect, we all make mistakes in life but we should learn from the past to heal the future. In conflict people demonstrate character not of their best traits, but it is character just the same. Again I retain memories that have to be willing to entertain as untrue and intend to believe a memory is true, simply because we remember the bad and do not focus on the positive. Blame is a very heavy burden to carry but for many years blaming others for your failure has an air of comfort about it. The process of exploring the past for pleasant memories may offset the bad memories. Being able to say I have not thought of that in years reminds you of the simpler aspect of the long standing connection you have had to your family. However, when you turn your mind to exploring the hidden nature of moments of conflicts; something in the body starts to go awry and the process can have powerful effects on your physical and psychological being. One may find oneself fidgety with efforts of mentally entering your childhood home may be blocking sudden desires to over eat, sleep, buy something you didn't need it, to bite your fingernails, to get a drunk. For many the desire and actions we often take, that the behavior becomes compulsive; before you have made a conscious decision to do so will find yourself in the kitchen eating whatever comes into view or on the phone talking to someone that will agree with your actions. We all want to hold on to our version of the truth. My daughter blames everyone else for her obesity! Her parents and her husband are the reason for her to be obese. She sometimes stops talking to us for a reason she generates in her mind. She has stayed away from us for periods of weeks or months at this very moment she is not answering my calls. The last time we had a conversation was eight days ago. I have to be very careful of what I say and how I say it when talking with my daughter or my wife. I accept that in the past I have been very sarcastic when talking to people especially my family. My nephew Frankie corrected me several times and I had to agree with him. The way he spoke to me was with a voice of love and not anger. Thru the years of meditation and Bible studies I have been blessed to be a better person. It was only when I had the maturity to accept my part in what happened that I was able first to have compassion for oneself and then to move forward toward my real self. Very few people are comfortable enough with who they are to be their truest self with their family, before a visit with my daughter for Thanksgiving dinner or Christmas. I prepared myself like if I was going into a battle ground. It is always the same routine it starts with my daughter and grand-daughter arguing with words of opinions and ends with my wife and me. In an effort to defend ourselves from others knowing our vulnerability we often create a false self that is powerful, unflawed and we think that we are perfect! Someone without weakness and therefore without humanity, this person is not someone with whom anyone in the family can be intimate, because there is no common point of connection no vulnerability for all the grandiosity of this false self. Therefore one must stay at an emotional distance from the family to preserve the imposing appearance concealing something inferior. The grandiose false self often externalizes accusations or abusive self destructive behavior disguised as rebellious fun – all defenses against facing the responsibility for change. This false self internalizes the anger, or defensiveness and maybe in a hidden depression or withdrawn in a fantasy world. When our false selves are in control, we are incapable of a person-to-person relationship with anyone in the family. The grand force self breezes through the family, offering advice and promising to help, imagining one can rescue everyone. However, it is not uncommon that this grand self is incapable of fulfilling any of these promises, because one has promised more than anyone can deliver. Looking back over the history of our families, most of us can see how we have at times played any number of variations on these basic false selves. The mask we choose is often based on a combination of factors including our inborn temperament, our mental capacities and the specific dynamics with the family as well as external circumstances. Through the mask of the false self we cannot see the family as it truly is nor can the family see or feel us. I went into exile because that's what God wanted me to do to write this revelation. It was not intended to erect a barrier between me and my family. To have breathing room during crisis between family and a time out in which to reflect and to refocus energy for a new approach to the problem. Time heals all wounds, this is not true, and time heals nothing. God is the only one that heals all wounds thru the "Holy spirit" Amen! Boundaries protect the authentic self allows you to remain calm, whole and lovingly detached in the face of conflict. The cooler we remain in conflict the better off we are. The false self always has something to prove to the family; either that the family was right about them or that the family was wrong! The real self has a healthy boundary between itself and the family knows when to assert itself. How to step back without anger and when to keep ones mouth silent, all owning others their successes or failures. The real self can say, I am and I love; without reciting a number of incidents that created or forced a distance. When you tell stories about why you are a stranger to your family, you bring with them the memory of a telling self. I suffered through especially painful and threatening childhood that tends to find reflection on my past difficulties. However, there is so much to be gained by escaping from the prison of our fetes and working through our feelings in the here and now! I have learned from meditation and reflection that what I originally viewed as a detriment came to have a decidedly profitable effect on my adult life. This shift in perspective is not an attempt to put too sunny a light on the past but is instead an attempt to allow me to hold both ideas simultaneously my fundamental strengths can often be generated by my family's weaknesses. My temperament was an aspect of my identity but few people are aware of the color of the lens with which we view the world. My thoughts of music, listening and meditation help me better understand my fundamental perspective on reality. Understanding the forces that shaped my family in present time and my role in future outcomes can make a profound change in the way I view the past. Today is Sunday, February 21, 2010 three days after my birthday. Today I had a telephone call early morning. This call was from a relative in Puerto Rico. This relative was telling me that in the internet there was an announcement that my oldest grand-daughter's was getting married. To me it was a big surprise. I told the relative that I didn't know anything about the event. To verify the news I called my grandson Justin her cousin. He was surprised that no one had said anything to me about it. Remembering and reflecting in the past takes a lot of willpower to contain the tears! Remembering when she was so little and I carried her in my arms and trying to teach her to sing. I have to detach from myself the idea of the truth and augment the memories and judgment I have carried with me for years to find compassion for those in the family who have caused us the most trouble. After liberating the past from my idiosyncratic suppositions, values and justifications I reflect on the idea that there are other equally valid perspectives of the same situations through re-framing oneself like a picture frame to allow your expectations to falter. After all these thoughts I spent this Christmas and New Year's 2009-2010 all alone in the apartment. I really believe God wanted me to do it, because I could have those days in Puerto Rico with my nephew Frankie and his wife Lucy invited me several times to go with them and not stay alone in the apartment. Every year we usually have Christmas dinner at our house on the 24th of December. Next day we all go to my youngest daughters' to open the presents. Imagine the excitement of you wrapping the gifts you are happy to give. The false smile of opening a present you did not want. The joy of Grandma and Grandpa surrounded by their legacy the dejection of the rebellious adolescent slumped by the couch. None of these moods alone describes the true holiday picture. Only by including all these images you can get a complete perspective on the family Holiday. I have found by analyzing my own self a situation in my family where a teenager attempts to extricate herself from a more fused family system. She begins to do some acting out drinking; taking drugs and becoming promiscuous an expression of anxiety that one desire for independence creates with the system. The teenager is then labeled by ones parents and the next of family as the problem child. In the family system approach, the child would be considered to be carrying the anxiety for the family system therapists would more likely treat one or both parents and not the teenager. Parental conflict is the way the family system balances the forces of togetherness and individuality. Conflicts grants both of the spouses emotional distance. This distance is however a negative solution as one still focuses on each other's world, but in a negative way. One already admitted ones defects and mistakes made with one's children when they were at home. That's all in the past; this is being written perhaps someone may still have the time to make positive changes in one's life. My wife blamed me for being too strict, overbearing and too rough with the discipline of our children. She called it child abuse, we blamed each other and continued to fight in front of the children one example of how we engaged in discussions and eventually ended up fighting. All three children were teenagers and would ask their mother; mom can we stay overnight with our friends, mom would reply its okay with me; ask your father! They came to me with a very happy face, dad, mom gave us permission to stay overnight at our friends house, is that okay with you! I would reply that is not okay! No! I would say to them then my wife would come to me, please let them go! We did not have a good family system and the children used one against the other. We continued to fight more frequently and eventually started retreating from the family unity. Today our children are married and we have good communication with me as long as I agree with them. Now that my daughters have their own families, they understand the importance of having a good family system of communicating with each other in a positive way. The past is the past! But sometimes by remembering the past it helps one be a better person. A triangle is not necessarily between three livings persons, a triangle can include someone who is deceased this triangle can exist with someone who is alive but you never take the time to talk and forget the past. It can exist within a person you hate, in other words, resentment is a way to continue to have a relationship with someone which is a form of negative intimacy. Anger is often a sign of the inability to forgive and let go of the past. People that constantly remember and live with the past are actually trying to hide their unacceptable feelings. These feelings are unconsciously a mechanism that helps oneself escape from the pain one's limitations to a more protected but unreal world. Our immature defenses protect us from being overwhelmed by a painful reality, but one keeps from adapting to the truth and facing reality. Crisis may not be gifts but they can be opportunities to see a larger truth about ourselves; though they may often feel more like punishment, denial is the drug of choice for many of us which are the defense one uses to ignore external reality. A husband believes that his wife really does love him, even though she has been unfaithful to him. In his immature state, he must deny the truth to protect his wounded sense of self. Which cannot afford to grasp the truth of one's infidelity if one acknowledges the truth one would be forced to change one's relationship or one would have to leave. His denial protects him from a change he may feel too weak to undertake and creates a false reality in which he can remain in the marriage. The more able one could function in reality which would help the outer worlds match. The more likely I am to depend on more mature defense mechanisms in times of trouble. Mature defenses can be learned by establishing a solid level of autonomy with our families. You have to have a defined and authentic sense of self learned to employ the more mature defenses. It is on these defenses that one relies on. These mature defenses are for the most part healthy ways to adapt, although they can be overused as altruism, the emphasis on service that many religious groups advocate. An age old practice and a healing mature defense although it is possible to neglect yourself in service to others. .Suppression defense is best defined as the delaying of gratification, if ones goal is losing weight, then learn to suppress ones desire for fatty foods. While one attempting to learn better eating and exercise habits. Anticipation; another mature defense may also be at play here as the anticipated feelings about weighing less and looking great adds to ones resolve to keep the compulsion to overeat to a minimum level. This action can direct a person to the mature defense of humor as ones defense! A person may take themselves serious and lapse from ones diet and making jokes about the end results for self healing. Humor teaches an important lesson about humanity and demonstrates the evolving nature of one. All defensive mechanisms are by definition unconscious and rarely used alone. Knowledge of them can be very important when we are trying to re-connect with our families, knowing that some painful or irrational behaviors are merely defensive mechanisms. This helps one to understand what goes on in the family and to accept it by being less personally. After a time defenses can become less protective and more constricting than necessary for survival. When our defenses barricade us or freeze us in time, we may close off from emotional growth and true connections with the family. Understanding that many of the actions others take are done to defend themselves are not necessarily conscious or personal; it is an important step in not being drawn into their emotional field. Understanding this allows us to stay connected to their fundamental humanity as well as our own without overreacting. By knowing the ultimate value of our own essential humanity and refusing to be provoked. We are much more likely to diffuse the conflict. There is no conflict if one doesn't engage. (There may be feelings to deal with however thru meditation and continuous prayers'). This helps us to keep our emotional channels clear through reflecting and re-framing, we come to understand or at least become open to the possibility that conflict in one's family was heavily influenced by forces that the individuals involved could not completely control. When one returns' to the family with an awareness of the defenses still existing there will be an opportunity to truly reconnect and being aware that many irritating actions are merely defenses. The many defenses your family members employ are for their own protection and not aimed specifically at hurting you. The defensive person may look strong, but in fact might feel cornered. He may be flailing internally grabbing at anything one can to keep others away, but is only in order to keep oneself. If one happens to strike you this is likely out of one's own weakness rather than personal malice. Defense mechanisms may be alternatives to worse behavior. The troubled person, who has caused oneself and the family a lot of heartache because of bad behavior, would seem as weak, a lunatic or disrespectful. The only chance we have to help this person is by prayer. The ability to listen without judgment and at the same time open strategy applies to interpersonal relationships as well. Angrily telling ones loved one that they may not marry a certain person or we will disown you, and you probably know that they will anyway! One should still tell them that you love them and respect their ability to make a choice. While also stating your truth by advising because of experience that they may not be the positive person for one's life. While there are a wide range of defensive tactics, probably the most common ones are most visible in our own families. The nagging criticism that parents perpetually make about ways in which ones disappointed them are in many cases projections of dreams they have for themselves and were never able to fulfill that because of all the good parents want for their children and they were never able to fulfill their own dreams. Sometimes we make comments to our children; like we wanted you to go to college. Your choice to get married with that so and so! Ones daughter is already married with her own family and she immediately retaliates with her defenses. Our comments would cause pain and for one to defend themselves, and the situation escalates into an argument or a temporary withdraw. Frequently when we want to correct an injustice we overcompensate. It always hurts both sides when a simple misunderstanding goes unresolved and becomes an argument. If you think you are misunderstood, most likely the person, who does not understand your point and feels the same way about you. This startling notion forces us to reconsider some of the basic disappointments that color our view of the family. Parents not understanding does not usually come from willful ignorance on ones part, but rather from the fact that they were projecting hopes and dreams that one might have and not take into consideration that the young adult has dreams of their own. The most insidious defense is to live in the myth of self sufficiency to pretend that we have no relationship with the family. Refusing to visit parents home is the form of denial that hurts the parents at all times. By this misunderstanding the child assumes a false assumption that the parents are not physically present in their lives and do not want a relationship with them. I once heard my children tell their mother that they would not want a relationship with me even if I came begging. The sad truth is they have a relationship either way whether they want to realize it or not and this relationship is a fantasy constructed of myth and mirrors the past. We can be anyone we want to be in our lives without having to face the messy reality. We can be the savior, sending home money and making a loving phone call. We can be the grandiose intellectual, too smart to need family or too busy with a demanding schedule to take time to just be with ones' family. We can be the lonely martyr – sadly stoic, ultimately heroic – sacrificing precious time with the family for a higher calling. From that distance, our family can be anything we need them to be as well, a family that fits our fantasized Hollywood version of ourselves. We can imagine them stuck in a time warp, forever lost in some childhood version of themselves, a symbolic shabby house, and full of conflicts that justify our continuous absence. We can romanticize a simple loving home where our absence is noted and we are pined for fantasy plus distance is a powerful defense, one that allows for a profound imaginary connection when the real connection, as we imagine it. By being too excruciating, boring, aggravating, sad, loving and to joyful to bear. What makes real connection to our family so full of violence, is that intimacy is messy, life is messy, we get sick, we act stupid, we fail at things, we hurt others and we get hurt ourselves. Yet, we cannot mythologize the traits or responses, or emotions we want from the families. When we are actually with them, only in present time can we get the real things, only in present time can we feel our father's or mother's love as unconditional as criticizing or as demanding or more likely as some combination of all three. Embracing the fullness of life encompassing the completeness, the humanity, the full catastrophe of another – is made possible only by being able to offer corresponding level of our own complex vulnerability and strength. In returning home after completing the mission God has given me during this year in exile, writing, meditation and prayer, I will be reconnecting with my family, choosing to be real. Knowing that by dropping our defenses, revealing our secrets and having the courage to tell our truth and hear the truth from the members of this family! The connection we long for will be real. Going home this time and in this manner, not only our past will be brand new but by the grace of God we would fulfill the happiness of a united, respecting and loving family. (Amen)

CHAPTER 9
FAMILY CODES

All families communicate in codes; my oldest daughter is an expert in family codes. Codes are shorthand that bonds the generations through an intimate language of shared meanings. When my daughter says Janay is pulling an Abby what my daughter means is that Janay is acting like her mother. A sister's remark, that her daughter is discovering her inner joy. They both understand the daughter has suddenly become just as particular about grooming and fashion as her mother, that while joy may have caused her daughter enormous grief in her childhood and adolescence with her strict expectations about appearance. By identifying her daughter's inner joy, she alludes to a struggle that only she and her brother know intimately. Both siblings acknowledge that they moved beyond the struggles with humor and humanity in this way. Codes close a circle around the family and these codes are also hidden in the moments of family conflict as the emotions in the moment cloud the intent or meaning of the messages one family member sends to another. For some people trying to find a sunny ending in the painful ways in which families cause trauma and insecurity can seem a glib denial of the damage done. One thing that has become clear to over time is that the family events have the meaning we give them. In many cases what we see is only what we are doing to ourselves. This is of course not the case of oppressive forms of abuse and neglect, but for most of us the estrangement from our families is not the result of actual violence. More often than not our anger at our families or our inability to be authentic stems from disappointment in ourselves. We often feel that they did not give us what we needed at some crucial moments or that they did not see and appreciate their parents for who they are at that moment in time, but the idea that things should be given to us is a child's view of the world. As adults we know very few things come our way just because we sit passively wanting them. It is always easier to focus on the conflicts within the family than to see through the conflicts to the deeper mystery of what the conflict says to you and about you. In most cases it is only later that we realize our disappointments stemmed from what we needed or wanted at that crucial moment. What we needed from the family then is what we need to find for ourselves now. Maturing is or should be the process of transforming from the powerlessness of a child to the power for an adult who understands what he needs and blames no one for his inability to understand. Victimhood keep us from seizing our fundamental power to make our own destiny or choosing to leave victimhood behind, then you begin to see your family as the laboratory for a new definition of yourself. This new self is defined through your struggles and through your intimate relationships. To really engage with your family in a struggle for a meaningful relationship requires you to ask yourself some fundamental questions. Why was I put on this earth? What am I here to learn? The answer to those questions is in the Bible. Before you were born, God planned the moment of your life, with free will so you make your choices. God wants us to discover the life he created for us to live here on earth to make our own choices to be defined by his commandments' and we might get to live forever in eternity with him. In the Bible, the book of Ephesians' 1:1 reads; it is in Christ that we find out who we are and what we are living for, long before we heard of Christ. He had his eyes on us, and designed us for glorious living, part of the overall purpose in his design for everything and everyone. (My personal opinion) If you really want to know why you were placed on this earth, you must begin by talking with God thru prayer.

I mentioned before about the book my daughter gave me for my birthday. This book is the only book beside the Bible that I have read more than once. The book was written by Rick Warren titled "The Purpose Living Life". I would like to quote some of his Bible quotations because one will understand why you were put here on this earth.

He states in his book; and I quote; the purpose of your life is for greater than your own personal fulfillment, your peace of mind or even your happiness. If you want to know the purpose of your life you have to begin at the right starting point. Focusing only in ourselves will never reveal our life's' purpose. The Bible says it is God who directs the life of his creatures; everyone's life is in his power. One must begin with God your creator. One exist only because God's will. You were made by God and for God and until you understand that, life will never make sense. It is only in God that we discover our origin, identity, meaning, purpose, significance and our destiny. God directs us for his purposes, not one using him for one's purpose. Christian books usually offer the same predictable steps to finding one's purpose; consider your dreams, clarify your values. Set some goals figure out what you are good at, aim high; go for it. Be disciplined and believe you can achieve your goals, involve others and never give up.

Of course these recommendations often lead to great success. You can usually succeed in reaching a goal if you put your mind to it. Being successful, fulfilling your life's purpose is not the same thing. You could reach all your personal goals becoming a raving success by the world standard, and still miss the purpose for which God created us. One needs more than self help, advice as the Bible reads; self help is no help at all, self sacrifice is the way, my way to finding yourself, your true self and sacrifice.

For thousands of years brilliant philosophers have discussed and speculated about the meaning of life. Philosophy is an important subject and has its uses but when it comes to determining the purpose of life, even the wisest philosophers are just guessing. Fortunately there is an alternative to speculation about the meaning and purpose of life. Its revelation is what God has revealed about life through his words of wisdom. The easiest way to discover the purpose of an invention is to ask the creator of it. The same is true for discovering your life's purpose; ask God, he has not left us in the dark to wonder and guess. He has clearly revealed his five purposes for our lives through the Bible. It is our owner's manual explaining why we are alive and how life works, what to avoid and what to expect in the future. It explains what self-help or philosophers', books could know. The Bible says God's wisdom ---- is not the latest message but more like the oldest. What God determined as the way to bring out his best in us. God is not just the starting point of one's life; he is the source of it. To discover your purpose in life you must turn to God's word. Not the world's wisdom, you must build your life in eternal truth not by psychology, success, motivation or inspirational stories. The Bible says it's in Christ that we find out who we are and what we are living for. Long before we heard of Christ and had our hopes up, he had his eyes on us, had designed us for glorious living. Part of the overall purpose is working out situations in everything. Right now you might be driven by a problem, and a pressure or a deadline. You may be driven by a painful memory a haunting fear or an unconscious belief. There are many circumstances, values and emotions that can drive ones' life. Some people spend their entire lives running from regrets and hiding their shame. Guilt driven people are manipulated by memories and they allow their past to control their future. They often unconsciously punish themselves by sabotaging their own success. When Cain sinned, his guilt disconnected him from God's presence. God said; you will be a restless wanderer on the earth. That describes most people today wondering through life without a purpose. We are products of our past, but we do not have to be prisoners of it. God's purpose is not limited by your past. He turned a murderer named Moses into a leader, and a coward named Gideon into a courageous hero. God can do amazing things with the rest of our lives.

The Bible says happiness for those whose guilt has been forgiven, what relieve for those who have confessed their sins and God has cleared their record. I have been for many years the recipient of resentment and anger! Some people hold on to hurt and never get over it. Instead of releasing their pain through forgiveness, they rehearse it over and over in their minds. Some resentment driven people "clam up" and internalize their anger while others blow up and explode on others. Both responses are unhealthy and unhelpful. Resentment always hurts one more than the other person, one resents. While one offender, has probably forgotten the offense and went on with his life. One continues to stew in their pain, perpetuating the past. Listen and think about it for a moment. Those who have hurt someone in the past cannot continue to hurt them, unless one holds on to the pain through resentment. Your past is past, nothing will change it and one is only hurting oneself with their bitterness. For one's own sake, learn from it and then let it go. The Bible reads, to worry about ones resentment would be a foolish, senseless thing to do! When you are driven by fear you miss a great opportunity because you are afraid to venture out. Instead they play it safe avoiding risks and trying to maintain the status quo. Fear is a self imposed prison that will keep one from becoming what God intends for one to be. One must move against it with the weapon of faith and love.

The Bible says well-established love, banishes fear since fear is crippling, a fearful life, a fear of death, that one hasn't fully formed their love. Driven by materialism, this drive to always want more is based on the misconceptions that having more will make one feel at piece, important, happier and more secure. But all three ideas are untrue because possessions provide temporary happiness. These things do not change; we eventually become bored with them and then want newer, bigger, better materialistic things. Your value is not determined by your valuables, God says the most valuable things in life are not materialistic things. One doesn't know all the keys to success, but a key to failure is to try to please everyone. You will tend to make choices based on circumstances, pressure and your mood at that moment. It is impossible to do everything people want of you. You just have enough time to do God's will. If you cannot get it done, it means you are trying to do more than God intended you to do.

The Bible says, a pretentious showy life is an empty life, a plain and simple life is a full life. It also leads to peace of mind and our Lord will give perfect peace to those who keep their purpose firm and put their trust in God. Many people are like gyroscopes' spinning around in a frantic pace but never going anywhere. Without a purpose, you will keep changing directions, jobs, relationships, churches, and most things attempted. One thinks that the next change will settle the confusion or fill the emptiness in your heart. You will spend far more time on the other side of death in eternity than you will here on earth. Here on earth is the preschool, the tryout for your life in eternity, as expressed by the Bible. This life is the preparation for the next. At most you will live a hundred years on earth, but you will spend forever in eternity. Your time on earth is a small parenthesis in eternity. The Bible says God has planted eternity in the human heart. You have an informed instinct that longs for immortality. This is because God designed you in his image to live for eternity. Even though we know eventually everyone dies. (The Authors opinion)!

Death always seems unnatural and unfair, and we feel we should live forever. One day your heart will stop beating. That will be the end of your body and your time on earth. But it will not be the end of you. Only, your spirit is just temporary residing in your earthly body. The Bible calls your earthly body a "tent" but refers to your future body as a "house" the Bible says when this tent we live in here on earth is torn-down God will have a house in heaven for us.

While life on earth offers many choices, eternity offers only two, heaven or hell. Your relationship to God on earth will determine your relationship to him in eternity. If you learn to love and trust God's son Jesus, you will be invited to spend the rest of eternity with the Lord. On the other hand if you reject his love, forgiveness and salvation you will spend eternity apart from God forever.

The most damaging aspect of contemporary living is short term thinking. To make the most of your life, you must keep the vision of eternity continually in your mind and the value of it in your heart. The Bible says, "No mere man has ever seen, heard or even imagined what wonderful things God has ready for those who love the Lord". However, God has given us glimpses of eternity in his words. In heaven we will be reunited with loved ones who are believers, released from all pain and suffering.

Just as the nine months I spent in my mother's womb were not the end in themselves but preparation for life so this preparation for the next life. If you have a relationship with God through Jesus you don't need to fear death. It is the door to eternity. It will be the last hour of your time on earth. But it will not be the last of you. (The Authors opinion). Rather than being the end of your life it will be your birthday into eternal life. The Bible says this world is not our home; we are looking forward to our everlasting home in heaven. The Bible offers three metaphors that teach us God's view of life; life is a test, life is a trust and life is a temporary assignment. These ideas are the foundation of how to live here on earth. Life's test is seen in stories throughout the Bible. God continues to tests people's character, faith, obedience, love, integrity and loyalty. Words like trials, temptation, refining, testing, occur more than two-hundred times in the Bible. God tested Abraham by asking him to offer his son Isaac. God tested Jacob when he had to work extra years to earn Rachel as his wife. Adam and Eve failed their test in the Garden of Eden, and David failed his test from God on several occasions. The Bible also gives as many examples of people who passed a great test such as Joseph, Ruth, Ester and Daniel. Character is both developed and revealed by tests, and all of life is a test. We don't know all the tests God will give us but we can predict some of them, based on the Bible.

Major changes, delayed promises, impossible problems, unanswered prayers, undeserved criticism, and even senseless tragedies. In my life I have noticed that God has tested my faith through tribulations. A very important test is how you acted when you cannot feel God's presence in your life. Sometimes God intentionally draws back, and we don't sense his closeness. The Bible says God withdrew from Hezekiah in order to test him and to see what was really in his heart. Hezekiah had enjoyed close fellowship with God, but at a crucial point in his life God left him alone to test his character, to reveal a weakness and to prepare him for more responsibility. The Bible says God keeps his promises and he will not allow you to be tested beyond your power to remain faithful. At the time you are put to a test, he will give the strength to endure and to provide you with obstacles'. My test was when my son Charlie died, he was the apple of my life and that pain will never go away, but I had to act strong for my loved ones. I felt pain beyond belief but that was my test, my son still lives in my heart!!! The Bible says, the world and all its possessions belong to the Lord, the earth and all who live on it are his. We really never own, anything during our brief stay on earth. God just loans the earth to us while we are here. It was God's property before you arrived and God will loan it to someone else after you die.

God created Adam and Eve, he entrusted the care of his creation to them as an appointed trustee of his property. The Bible says, God blessed them, who have many children, so your descendants will live all over the earth and bring it under their control. I am putting you in charge of everything one enjoys and is to be treated as a trust that God has placed in your hands. The Bible says; what you have, God has given you, why boast as though you have accomplished something on your own!

Christians live by a higher standard, so we must take care of the little we do have. The bible says, those who are trusted with something valuable must show they are worthy of that trust. At the end of your life on earth you will be evaluated and rewarded according to how well you handled what God entrusted to you. If you treat everything as a trusted reward from God, first you will be given God's affirmation; he will say "Good Job! Well done! Next you will receive a promotion and be given greater responsibility in eternity.

I always talk about having respect for money; People fail to realize that money is both a test and a trust from God. God uses finances to teach us to trust in him, for many people money is the greatest test of all. God watches how we use money to test how trustworthy we are, which will help us with the true riches of heaven. How one manages their money, determines how much God can trust you with spiritual blessings and "true riches", Jesus said from everyone who has been given much, much will be demanded. For the one who has been entrusted with much, much more will be asked! Life is a test, trust in the Lord for he gives to us of himself.

"Lord, remind me how brief my time on earth will be, remind me that my days are numbered and that my life is fleeing away". (Psalms 39:4)

"I am here on earth for just a little while". (Psalms 119:19)

Life on earth is a temporary assignment. The Bible is full of metaphors that teach about the brief temporary transient nature of life on earth. Life is described as a mist breath, and a wisp of smoke.

The Bible says, for we were born but yesterday….Our days on earth are as transient as a shadow. To make the best use of your life, you must never forget two truths; first, compared with eternity, life is extremely brief; second, earth is only a temporary residence. You will not be here long, so don't get too attached. Ask God to help you see life on earth as he sees it. David prayed, Lord help me realize how brief my time on earth will be. Help me to know why, I am here for but a moment. We use terms like alien, pilgrim, foreigner, strangers, visitors and traveler to describe our brief stay on earth. David said, "I am but a foreigner here on earth" and Peter explained, "if you call God your father, live your time as a temporary resident on Earth".

This is the month of March 2010 I have been at the apartment for six months. I signed a lease for one year this is one of my temporary residences here on earth. I have been meditating, praying and reading the Bible every day, sometimes as many as four times per day. I have never in my life felt so free and relaxed until now. My sister-in-law Josephine has been reading the Bible for the last fifty years, and is a very spiritual person. We talk to each other every weekend, sometimes for as much as two hours. We talk a lot about the world news on television. We also talk about what is happening in the United States and in many parts of the world. We both agree, what is happening in the world is written in the Holy Bible. In the book of exodus 4:11-12, God said; "Who has made man's mouth? Or who makes the mute, the deaf, the seeing or the blind? Have not I, the Lord? Now therefore go and I will be with your mouth and teach you what you shall say" Whenever you wonder what God could possibly have been thinking when he called someone like you to such an extraordinary adventure of faith, remember an ageing shepherd with a bad temper and a batched record. His name was Moses, one of the Old Testament's greatest leaders. He was the most reluctant with the Lord; his story started in the outback of Median a desolate region to the east of the Sinai, Peninsula. After an earlier promising start as an adopted son in the courts of Pharaoh, things go downhill fast. One day he happens upon an Egyptian master beating an Israelite. Enraged and thinking no one was looking. Moses kills the Egyptian and buries him in the sand. The next day when he tries to separate two scuffling Israelites, one of them says, who made you ruler and judge over us? Are you thinking of killing me as you killed the Egyptian, (Exodus 2:14) feeling rejected by his own people and exposed as a murderer, Moses flees. For forty years he hides in the desert herding sheep and a man on the run from failure and shame. But God still has plans for Moses. One day God speaks to him out of a burning bush, and what he presents is a challenging proposition; I will send you to Pharaoh that you may bring my people, the children of Israel and out of Egypt, (Exodus 3:10). In view of his circumstances and past record Moses response is understandable. "Who am I?" he asked. God's extraordinary future for him has thrown him into a full scale identity crisis. (Do you recognize that reflex?) God plants a seed in your Spirit with an unusual exciting plan to be a tool in the Lords name. You see for example, others who succeed seem to have that ability you don't have, you see what it would take in personal sacrifice. You see your own sorry existence, questionable past, difficult personality and rusty skills.... Why would God's extraordinary plans for you throw you into an identity crisis? If you look at the account of the conversation between Moses and God (Exodus 3-4), you will see Moses putting up one objection after another to the Lord even though the Lord has plans for him to be completed;

Who am I that I should go?
Who am I that I should lead?
Who will I that sent me?
What if they don't believe me?

After telling God that he was disqualified because he wasn't a good talker, Moses' defense with a desperate plea; Oh Lord, please send someone else, to do it. Still God persist and prevails this is an identity crisis and it is the defining moment in Moses life. You see, all his questions and concerns are good ones and all of his feelings of inadequacy are real. But yet after Moses says yes, God uses this shy reluctant sheepherder to accomplish one of the most amazing leadership feats in History. If you haven't arrived at this turning point you will, one day! God's miraculous kingdom works through you. God will have to call your past the truth about yourself and show that what really matters is the truth about him. He will tell you as he did to Moses; "I am God". "I am sending you, I will never forsake you, and this is the beginning of your new identity an unlikely hero whose God is strong, loving, trust worthy enough to accomplish anything I call you to do". When Christ called the apostle Paul, he never looked back, from his Spiritual journey, with few distractions and compromises, he could tolerate any challenge. Listen to his testimony near the end of his life: "Whatever was my profit, now considered losses for the sake of Christ, one thing I do; forgetting what is behind and striving towards what is ahead. Continuing goals in Christ Jesus name. (Philippians 3; 7, 13-14).

How can you and I keep our hearts devoted and our legacy safe? Learning from Paul's advice, summarizing a lifelong plan of action into three simple commitments; Keep Christ first in our thoughts and actions: Press ahead toward God's goal for our life's: Let the past go!

CHAPTER 10
UNDERSTANDING GENEROUS LOVE

When God calls, your response my friend should be to follow his path until your last breath; you will never fully know the dimensions of his generous love and important purpose for you. Strive towards the Lord by praying to him and forgetting everything else. If we keep this loyalty to God in our hearts, soon we will be standing before his throne. With great anticipation we will hear God say "Well done, my good and faithful servant, enter into the joy of your Lord". The Bible says, we are the Lords ambassadors, sadly many Christians have betrayed their king and his kingdom. They have foolishly concluded that because we are here on earth it's our home. The "Bible is clear". Friends this world is only a temporary place, do not indulge your ego at the expense of your soul. God warns us to not get too attached to what's around us because it is temporary. We are told, those in frequent contact with the things of the world should make good use of them without becoming attached to them for this world and all it contains will pass. We are preparing for something even better, the things we see now are here today, gone tomorrow but the things we cannot see now will last forever. In order to keep us from becoming too attached to earthly possessions. God allows us to feel a significant amount of discontent and dissatisfactions in life, these obstacles are the Lords challenges.

Earth is not our final home; we were created for something much better. A fish would never be happy living on land, because it was made for water. An eagle could never feel satisfied if it wasn't allowed to fly. It is a fatal mistake to assume that God's goal for one's life is material prosperity or popular success as the world defines it. The abundant life has nothing to do with material abundance and faithfulness to God;

he does not guarantee success in a career or even in ministry. Never focus on temporary crowns. John the apostle was faithful, but he was beheaded. Millions of faithful people have been martyred and have lost everything, or have come to the end of life with nothing to show for it. The end of life is not the end...

This is the year 2010, we all know if you watch the news on television so many things are happening in this world, Earthquakes', tsunamis, hurricanes and still more to come according to the Bible. Millions of people have lost their homes, this is the United States of America the most powerful country in the world but still people are sleeping, and living in their cars. Unemployment is out of control, and all these things are happening and we have no control over these events.

Signs of the end of age, "I believe the war in Iraq will be terminated, troops are coming home in the year 2012. Unemployment will level off to a normal rate, but things are yet to come. I believe that two women will attempt to run for president and Vice President of the United States of America. The Republicans are calling President Obama a one term President. They don't realize that they are politicians with an agenda to work for people that put them in office.

Saturday, March 7, 2010 I went to the grocery store to buy a few items that I needed. I stopped by my house to see my wife to pick up the junk mail. She handed me a letter from a married couple, which was interested on buying our house. The letter was addressed to my name only. She said here is this letter; these people are interested in purchasing our home. My wife forgot that I cannot sell the house because God gave us this home as a temporary shelter here on earth. She forgot about the vision I had in Puerto Rico up on the mountain back in January 1999. I had the vision four month after the last Hurricane. We survived four Hurricanes while we were living in Puerto Rico.

In the year 2012 in the month of September there will be disasters, the biggest Hurricane in History, Florida, Dominican Republic, Haiti, Cuba and Puerto Rico. The United States troops will be out of Guantanamo Bay before the disaster. In the same year Iraq will become a democracy. Ezekiel 7:23, the Lord said; "prepare chains, because the land is full of bloodshed and the city is full of violence. I will bring the wicked of the nation to take possession of their houses. I will put an end to the pride of the mighty and their sanctuaries will be desecrated.

When terror comes they will seek peace but there will be none. Calamity upon calamity will come and rumors upon rumors. They will try to get a vision from the prophet the teaching of the law by the priest will be lost as will the council of the elders. The king will mourn, the prince will be clothed with despair and the hands of the people of the land will tremble. I will deal with them according to their conduct and by their own standards. I will judge them today Jesus said; and is written in the Holly Bible, John 14:15:27, Jesus promises the Holy Spirit, "You love me,, you will obey what I command and I will ask the Father and he will give you another counselor to be with you forever – the Spirit of truth the word cannot accept him, because it neither sees him nor knows him, but you know him, for he lives within you. And will be in you, it will not leave you. I will come to you, before long, the world will not see me anymore, but you will see me, because I live and you also will live. On that day you will realize that I am in my Father and you are in me and I am in you. Whoever has my commands and obeys them will be the one that loves me".

Today with so many years of experience in life and with the help of the Holy Spirit, I can see life differently than I did years ago. Now I am more relaxed and accept, challenges in life. As a family there are many challenges as something that God allows to happen for a purpose. Family emotions are complicated by the transmission of signals. At family gatherings, each person's emotions change with the pressures that come from the clash of the different energies. Family members bring with them different moods, and when they walk into a room you can feel the mood change; it is as impractical as the weather. We have all been in houses where the air is dry as a dusty sandal or the atmosphere is as chilly as a snowfall. Individual energies swirl and blend. Storms build and disperse; low level depressions and cold fronts separate us from each other. Communicating through this is often as difficult as trying to get a clear signal from one cell phone to another. God knows that I have tried to have a good honest relationship with my wife and two daughters. There is only one problem; it is called the past! They cannot let go of the past I am being reminded over and over of my misdeeds. If you are depressed and you are still holding onto the past, understanding your own state of mind compels you to maintain those challenges. Being, understood and releasing the thoughts of the past should bring forth harmony with one another.

Between adults, resentment is often a sign that brings ill feelings, there should be listening not hearing, by both parties in order to understand not to disagree.

When you think of being in love, the last persons thought of, are your family members. The kind that is supported by ancient myths in romantic love, you are attracted to someone who matches your interests, values and tastes. In this style of love you orchestrate the interaction with active pursuit, fantasies, and if it is to succeed long term, working to maintain the relationship is a must. When it is working particularly in the beginning you feel unknown, unseen and non-understood. With many love affairs, when you break up it's over. With families it never ends. Love in the family is less specific, if asked; most people would likely say of course I love my family. In most cases, it would be embarrassing to admit anything short of love for them unless they are dangerous or destructive people. Kicking doors and walls are the ways individuals get rid of frustrations. I no longer need to defend myself about the lost years because they are over. We make mistakes and have to keep our focus positively not on resentments, and learn to take a time out if things get rocky. All my life I have been a positive, proud and working person. Pride is one's, emotion that should be understood to continue in a positively direction.

These painful feelings overcome us when we are to blame for something bad. Pride is the opposite; we are to blame for something good. As one of the so called seven deadly sins, pride has a mixed reputation. Pride makes people swell, and before a fall, an emotion can go too far and perhaps this is especially true for pride. When specifically and tempered with appropriate humility, pride is clearly a positive emotion. Pride blooms in the wake of an achievement, with your effort and skills for success. It is that good feeling you get when you put the finishing touches on a home improvement project whether is fixing the washing machine, planting a garden, or redesigning your kitchen. When you achieve something in school or at work, aced a test, wins a race, made a sale or published your ideas one would feel pride in ones accomplishments'.

One Sunday about a year ago, the pastor of the church where we go, talked about pride, and he said that Christians are not suppose to be proud because this is the same as being arrogant. I am not the type of Christian to get into a discussion about religion or politics; I let God be the judge to that. You are proud when you recognize that you made a difference to someone else, through your help, kindness or guidance. These are not any achievements but socially valued ones. We sense a deep level that our actions will be valued by others. That is what makes pride a self conscious emotion. Unless you are a sociopath, you are actively aware of how your actions – good or bad – can be perceived by others. You feel pride when you are praiseworthy and guilt whom you are blameworthy. Pride carries with it the urge to share the news of your achievements with others, either in words, "hey, look what I did", gestures (upright posture), head tilted slightly back, slight smile , hands on hips, arms raised in victory or both. I wrote at the beginning of this book about the years working at the chemical companies. From 1951 to 1984, now that I am much older I realize and see why I was successful at every project assigned. Those years I was young and never paid attention to the word pride, but yet, I was proud to accomplish and achieve what I was being paid for.

When we felt God speak to us in prayer, the Lord had a plan for the Church, with the Holy Spirit, to start working towards three services on Sunday for Church, which was the goal intended. We will work for this goal until we draw our last breath. Until the moment you pass into eternity, you will never know the dimensions of his generous love and important purpose for us. The Bible says, in Corinthians 1:26-29; brothers, think about what you were when you were called. Many of you were wise by human standards, many were influential, and many were of noble birth. But God chose the foolish things of the world to shame the wise; he chose the lovely things of this world and despised things that are not to nullify things to boast before him. I will go anywhere provided it is forward!

The mindscape of pride is expansive as well it kindles dreams for further and larger achievements in similar domains; pride fuels the motivation to achieve. When I was working with chemicals and the chemists came to me with a problem in the production area, I always told them, never give up put your heart in what you are doing. You are being paid for what you are doing, keep trying in the laboratory and persist until you achieve your goals. After succeeding subordinates, would come to me, with a big smiles and thank me for the support, and one could see the pride the subordinates showed on their' faces.

Our son passed away on October 4, 1974 in a car accident. Up to this day 36 years later, I am blamed for his death. I asked my wife for forgiveness, the Bible says, for if you forgive man, when they sin against you, your heavenly father will also forgive you. But if you do not forgive man of their sins your father will not forgive your sins. When you are at peace with god, you are blessed forever. (Believe me I know). Closely related to inspiration things happen when you come across goodness on a grand scale. You literally feel overwhelmed by greatness. By comparison you feel small and humble which makes you stop in your tracks. You are momentarily transfixed in boundaries that melt away and feel part of something larger than yourself. Mentally you are challenged to absorb and accommodate the sheer scale of what you have encountered. Sometimes we are awed by nature, as with stunning sunsets at the grand canyon or by seeing hearing and feeling the power of the ocean waves smashing and wearing away at the rocky cliffs. Other times we are awed by humanity as when we see people specially children dying during an earthquake or a fire. Although positivity at times sits so close to the edge of safety that we get a whiff of negativity as well as mixes with fear when we have witnessed four Hurricanes or seen the world trade center towers collapsed. Like gratitude and inspiration is a self transcendent emotion. It compels us to see ourselves as part of something much larger. Whether it's God's creation or this nation's great progress, one can also bind up emotionally to powerful and charismatic leaders who often seem larger than life. "Love"

My thirty five years old grandson, Justin; who traveled with us in the early 80's, is a man and is still living with grandma and grandpa. He is a single father, and my wife and I look at him like our son Charlie! I talked to him one late evening; he was surprised because I never call him late at night. I talked to him as a mentor to think about getting married and about his future, by having personal goals in his life. To be, an achiever, to have a job with benefits. Explained to him about having his own place to learn how to have responsibilities and not depend on anyone! One thing that we admire about him is that he is very respectful. After talking with him he said thanks for the advice grandpa. I replied think about it; you are old enough to make your own decisions. I will respect your final decision and God bless you! I pray that someday I will be able to talk to my granddaughter the same way I talk to my grandson.

I have been a mediocre and authoritarian father. Thank God, they make me very happy when they admit that I have been a good provider. (Let God be the superior judge), being a very positive person all my life and having trust in God and doing what the Holy Spirit puts in my heart. Today at eighty years of age, I feel great, mentally and physically. I am prepared to answer the father in heaven when he asks me the two questions. Positivity can be described in many ways, in longing to embrace loved ones.

Laughing and sharing with a neighbor as you watch your kids acting silly. It is the memories you hold for your future, and seeing them in their future education. Positivity can be found everywhere. I believe whether you experience positivity or negativity depends vitally on how you think. We have the power to turn positivity on and off for ourselves. I pray for people when they ask me or when I am aware of the necessity of prayers for the situation, but I still pray. Not all prayers are answered because the positive switch on both sides is turned off. Sometimes at church you see the same brothers and sisters every Sunday come forward to pray. But in my case and I included my wife, we believe that the proper way to solve a problem or a sickness is by looking first at the situation analyze it and then decide if you have control over the problem. Positive emotions, like all emotions – arise from how you interpret events and ideas as they unfold. Whether you allow yourself to take a moment to find the good and when you have found it, you build on that goodness and let it grow.

Creating more positivity in your life is not simply a matter of wishful thinking but practicing correct feelings for specific situation that arise and correct thinking to make a positive conclusion to any problem!

CHAPTER 11
PRAYING & MEDITATING

Friday 12, 2010 4:00 a.m. the garbage truck came to pick up the garbage from the apartment building complex; the dumpster is situated right across the street from my bedroom window. The trucks motor would make loud noises and would wake up most of the neighborhood. Every Friday after the truck leaves I sit at the edge of my bed and close my eyes. I elevate my thoughts to the sky and go into a trance like a dream but I am wide awake.

God, the son and the Holy Spirit, directed me to the Bible, the book of Isaiah Chapter I:1: 31 God said; *"hear O' heaven, listen, O'earth, for the Lord has spoken; "I rear children and brought them up but they have rebelled against me, the ox knows his master, the donkey, his owners, but Israel does not know my people do not understand oh sinful nation, a people loaded with guilt a group of evildoers, children given to corruption. They have forsaken the Lord; they have spurned the Holy one, of Israel and turned their backs on him".*

Today is Saturday early morning while saying my prayers and meditating I thought about my brother-in-law Felix. I started dialing his telephone number, I wanted to talk to him because the last time I talked to him was six months ago before I moved into the apartment. The telephone rang several times and there wasn't an answer, I remember that he and his wife observe the Sabbath. They follow the Law of Moses and they do not eat certain meats because according to the Old Testament they are unclean food. Felix visited us when we lived in Puerto Rico, my wife was cooking rice, beans and pork chops. He refused to eat because he said that the pork was unclean food. My wife asked him if he wanted to eat the rice and beans. He said no because you put bacon in the beans. I jokingly said well, if you get hungry go outside and eat bananas. I respect his belief, but as a Christian I follow Jesus teaching. I worship the father, the son and the Holy Spirit.

The Bible says in Matthew 12:1-12: *"At the time Jesus went through the grain fields on the Sabbath; his disciples were hungry and they began to pick some heads of grain and eat them. When the Pharisees saw this; they said to him; look, your disciples are doing what is unlawful on the Sabbath; he answered, haven't you read what David did when he and his companions were hungry; he entered the house of God and his companions ate the consecrated bread which was not lawful for them to do; but only for the priests, or haven't you read on the law that on the Sabbath the priest's in the temple desecrate the day and yet are innocent. I tell you that one greater than the temple is here. If you had known what these words mean;* "desire mercy not sacrifice. *You would not have condemned the innocent for the son of man is Lord of the Sabbath. He said to them if any of you has a sheep and it falls into a pit on the Sabbath, will you not take hold of it and lift it out of the pit. How much more valuable is a man than a sheep; therefore it is lawful to do good on the Sabbath, Jesus said; What goes* into a man's mouth does not make him unclean, but what *comes out of his mouth, that is what makes him unclean". "The things that come out of the mouth come from the heart and this makes a man unclean".*

For out of the heart comes false testimony and false accusations even from your own family. When you communicate with your soul, your higher self is calling. This is called the higher – self experience. Your full potential is calling you; you felt the possibilities of what you can be and that helps you become those possibilities. By understanding your higher self one lives their full potential each moment. They are delighted with life; they think, speak and act consciously; they care for life and respect it. My nephew Frankie, when he sees me or talks to me on the phone, first thing he says; uncle life is good! That indicates that he is in communication with his soul continually. Sometimes this called waking in your life becomes your higher self, to communicate with your soul at all time.

The creator gathered all of the creation and said I want to hide something from the humans until they are ready for it. (The opinion of the author). It is the knowledge that they create their own reality. The book, (The Purpose Driven Life) by Rick Warren has this quote. *"Give it to me, said Salomon; I will hide it in the bottom of the ocean. No, said the creator; one day they will go to the bottom of the ocean and they will find it! Give it to me said the bear. I will take it into the mountains, "no" said the creator. One day they will dig into the mountains, and they will find it! Give it to me said the eagle. I will take it to the moon. They will never find it, no said the creator. One day they will go to the moon and they will find it even there. Then grandma mole rose; everyone became quiet; they know that although she has no physical eyes, grandma lives with the breast of mother earth, and sees with spiritual eyes. Put it inside them she said. It is done; said the creator now we have discovered the secret".*

Using multisensory perception requires looking inside you. How could you ever find the secret with your five senses? You could not; they are designed to look outward. Everything that they detect is outside of you, even when your body hurts, it hurts because something outside of you; like some food that you ate, or a hammer that you hit your finger; eating different foods and keeping the hammer away from your finger; solve the problems. This is how we have learned to solve problems, in many occasions I have told my wife that my mind helps to alleviate pain and discomfort in one's body. The five senses provide information about things that are outside of you; one thinks about that information and then acts differently – maybe if one could create the same consequences, like hurting your finger. When you make the connection between the hammer and your finger and your pain one changes the way you do things. Now that we are becoming multisensory, we have information about what happens inside of us, as well as what happens outside of us. Insights and hunches become part of the picture. If you take into account only what happens outside of you; then you are not seeing the right picture.

When my two daughters stopped speaking to me – first I was sad but not angry, I said to myself, perhaps they have a reason. It felt that they were being unfair to me. But then I looked back on it and realized that happens to everyone. When you realize that everything that happens to you is for your own good. You are seeing your life the way your soul sees it. Even if what happens is painful like the death of a son or being abused, you can still realize even while it is happening, it is for your good if you practice thinking this way. You will save yourself a lot of fear and pain as I could have done during my younger days.

This is a new way of reasoning, not like most people reasoning in the old days because natural perception allows one to see what happens, every moment is perfect, no matter what it is. Most importantly one should bless everyone at all times or pray for them. Think about blessing all people you meet because of their smile, gentleness and personality; which may be a mother, nurse or someone who makes people feel good about them-selves. You cannot bless and judge someone if they are treating you unfairly or rudely, trying to hurt you with words; if you really want to bless everyone you meet, you have to bless people like this also!

Here is another emergency blessing that you can use. Say to yourself, this person is bringing me a lesson that is very important for me to learn. If it were not for this person I might not be able to understand the wrong or right of the situation. One day I remember talking to my daughter (no names) on the phone, she was very upset with her sister, which is usually a happening with siblings. One of them wanted to apologize and ask for forgiveness of the other sisters misunderstanding. Instead of us having a positive conversation, it became a confrontation instead of correcting a problem it created another! She unloaded on me very drastically, I tried to reason with her but she was not listening to understand, instead to disagree. I think it is still a positive situation with the disagreement of the conversation, because I feel good that my daughters still come to me for advice and I make a negative situation positive for me! My maturity level, at this time in my life is to understand what is happening, instead, of in the past of my authoritarian position, now I have learned to listen to understand!!!!

Today is Sunday March 14, 2010 tomorrow is my oldest daughter's birthday. All I can do is to ask God to bless her and take care of her. I visited my wife early morning and she was happy to see me (by the glory of God). I told her God willing, I will finish writing this manuscript this month and then I will be moving back home. Changes in my way of being and my maturity level have helped me to be more understanding of the situations created by me by the way I use to answer my family. Sometimes I see a movie which plays out the same, a beginning, during and end of the movie. I virtually realize that life is sometimes like a movie, me being the main character, where realities shift from one script to another in a moment. When you make a decision the virtual reality is a feeling of satisfaction. Whatever you decide causes something to happen. That is also what it feels like to have part of your own basic human needs of happiness. All persons have their own likes and dislikes. If you do not know about them you will suddenly find yourself liking or disliking your actions. Most people have short comings that they do not know about and should learn and understand! Ones' obsessions, compulsions, and addictions, are so strong that if you do not control them, negative results are inevitable.

People that are hooked with alcohol or drugs are deceiving themselves with the feelings that are created through their own addictions. They cannot stop because they are completely without power over themselves. One creates feelings of fear, uselessness, inadequacy and depressions and others can recognize those feelings. Until you recognize your own inadequacies, you continue with your moods and tendencies. But it does not surprise you anymore, you find yourself getting angry without a reason and not knowing why. You must take charge of your feelings, as the Buddhist's say "there are eight winds, they are gains and losses, praises and ridicules, credits and blames and suffering and joy. If you are not aware of them; they will blow you away like dry leaves in an autumn breeze". When someone praises you, and you are being blown away by the wind of praise it affects everyone differently. "*One day in ancient China a young man thought he had become enlightened. He wrote a poem to his master about how he was not affected by the eight winds. Then he sent it to his master – who lives three hundred miles up the Yangtze River. When the master read the poem, he wrote "Fart, Fart" on the bottom and sent it back. The more the young man read those words, the more upset he got. At last he decided to visit his master. In those days, a three hundred mile trip up the Yangtze River was a very difficult journey. As soon as he arrived he went straight to his master's temple. Why did you write this, he asked bowing? Does not this poem show that I no longer have been blown about by the eight winds? You say that you are no longer blown about by the eight winds! Replied the master, but two little farts blew you all the way up here! The young man could not stop being angry until he discovered how much he hurt. A lot of winds were blowing him around to the point of making that trip*".

This is what happens when you are not aware of what you are feeling. One thing I always tell my daughters and my grandchildren:

125

Making choices is the most powerful thing that you do in your life. Choices liberate and imprison; they create illness, health problems and usually everything you do are your choices. By you doing nothing is making a choice! Are you able to choose what you do next? Or is your choice always made for you! My wife asked me the other day; do you still have the pain on your buttocks. I have had that pain for almost a year. She knows that I am not the type of person to see a doctor, unless I think it is absolutely necessary. So I told her that pain is gone. She asked; what did you do? I replied I am not eating red meat anymore. She said, I have the same pain now; well stop eating red meat, I replied. "That is the power of choice" Each choice creates an action negative or positive which helps create a future! It brings into being one of many possible future dreams. That is the future that you will live, for example you may decide not to go to college to further your education. Then you decided to get married to someone that did not finish High School but drives a fancy car. Because of that decision you will meet people you did not know and understand the influences they have on you. You will learn new ways of understanding that the future is different from if one would have completed college. You chose your future moment by moment.

You do this whether you are aware of it or not. That is what happens, when you do not know about choosing the correct passage to your future. This again is your choice your every action dictates the positive or negative results of your life. An, intent is not a wish; a wish does not cause anything to happen. Choices are the way things determine ones' life.

Remember for every action there is an equal opposite reaction. You can see what your intensions are by looking at what is happening around you. Your attitude creates everything you experience. For example; if you play baseball your intensions are not the game, but to win! Your attitude will change depending on the outcome of winning or losing. You will look forward to playing relaxed and ready for anything that develops. One is anxious before each game. If one loses, that action is not satisfying, and your teammates have the same feelings. Now if your team did their best and still loses, the feeling is not gratifying but the loss is easier to understand! With a positive attitude of the outcome of the game, losing or winning creates your thought process for understanding ones feelings of self needs. It is ones choice, to make these results positive or negative.

When you intend to create harmony, cooperation, sharing and reverence for life, your intentions and the intentions of your soul are the same. When you become authentically powerful, creating authentic power is a process. Each time you choose harmony, cooperation, sharing or reverence for life. You challenge yourself to achieve personal goals.

"Forgiveness and Harmony" Some people forgive but do not forget. I know some people that constantly bringing the past up especially during family gatherings. They do not seem to get the message when I leave as soon as the negative conversation begins. Forgiveness' and harmony go together. When you forgive someone, nothing stands between you and that person. Even if there is friction with personal friends, acquaintances, or even family member; forgiveness should still be the end results.

Feelings of harmony in ones life, does not mean harmony with other people although that is a plus. Negative feelings create anger, but that anger is your choice, and one is the blame for that anger. It might of occurred without ones action, understanding, or believe, but the end results is yours! This is how one create harmony it is also how you forgive.

May 6, 2010, is sixty years of marriage for my wife and I. I remember last year I went to the florist. I said to the florist I want the best flowers you have, specially the roses. Every flower here is the best, replied the florist. There was a young man there looking for the same flowers. He asked me; how long have you have been married. I replied 59 years and he said; this is my first year I hope I last that long. I said; if you give and take with respect, understanding, misunderstandings, and rough times, love will conquer everything. Your marriage will last and you might be explaining the same as we are talking, to a young person in the future. Problems and bad times can happen anytime whether you are young or old. As he left he turned around and said thank you sir, for talking to me!

When you see even for a moment that something is special, maybe the real thought is clarity. Clarity is seeing that everything and every person are special no matter what or who it is. I remember a Navajo prayer that reads; "Beauty in front of me, beauty behind me, all around me beauty" This is very different from in the thought process of most people seeing their lives develop. Most people think that their experiences are more beautiful than others, and that some people are more special than others.

Which way is real? Imagine walking along a beach on a foggy day. You cannot see very far, and one hears the waves crashing on rocks seagulls singing and the wind blowing. Cold penetrates your clothes and you shiver, even if it's wet and gray. Sounds come from places you cannot see and you are frightened. This happened to me when I was a young boy in Puerto Rico. Now imagine you are walking on the same beach and the sun is shining, sunlight sparkles on the water. Gulls fly through a cloudless sky, cliffs with wild flowers tower above. Your feet sink into the warm sand, clarity is seeing without the fog. It is getting your bearing in a well lighted landscape. Like seeing without restrictions and, almost all of us have feared the night, at one time or another, crying with the feeling of loneliness! When we realize where we are, exchanging a frightening experience in the dark for a wholesome experience in the light. When you see clearly everyone and everything is special. So each time you share you learn to see clearly, the more you do it the better it becomes. When you share a positive feeling it is the best gift you can give.

When you give gifts like these you start to receive them in return as the Bible says. After a while everything that you give seems as you receives a gift from above. The trees and the mountains are also gifts. Who gave the animals, birds and you life? These are gifts from the creator, along with experiences that are perfect for you. This gift comes each moment from the time that you were in your mother's womb until you die. That is how you and the universe work together. Each moment you choose a new gift and when the time comes you will receive the beauty that the universe offers. You do this by setting your intentions and then acting on them. Everyone gets what he or she ordered. If you order fear, you will get fear. If you order love, then love is what you get. When; your order is filled the universe shares with you. Complaining about ones gifts is walking in a fog. Recognizing your gifts and who ordered them is walking in the sunshine. Walking in the sunshine is clarity. "Love is everywhere you look" Love is inside and outside the cells in your body. Your blood loves your heart and your lungs. Your spine loves your brain. Your body is a love story that continues day after day. You are a walking and talking love story and this story ends' when we pass on. The love stories happen whether we see them or not, ending when the tree falls, a new chapter begins. The tree decays and gives all of itself worth back to the earth; insects devour it and birds eat the insects. Bees make hives in it and bears eat the honey from the hives. Even when the tree disappears the story is not over. More trees appear and more insects, birds and animals are part of the life that continues. When the forest disappears the story does not end, but affects all the participants of the forest. Love and reverence go together. You are part of their suffering, happiness and part of their story.

That is the love unconditionally given to us and received from the Lord. The Lord wired us with five senses and emotions so one can experience it. He wants us to enjoy life not just endure it. The reason you are able to enjoy pleasures on earth is that God has allowed us to have emotions. The Bible tells us that God grieves, gets jealous, angry and feels compassion, pity, sorrow and sympathy as well as happiness.

Our payment to the Lord is instructed through "worship", reading the Bible, and the lord is pleased only with those who worship him and trust in his love.

Anything that brings pleasure to God is an act of worship. Like a Diamond, worship is multifaceted. It would take volumes to cause all there is to understand about worship, but we will look at the primary aspects of worship. Jesus said, the father seeks worshipers and depending on your religious background, you may need to expand your understanding of worship. One may think of church services with singing, praying and listening to a sermon or thinking of ceremonies, candles and communion, or healing, miracles and ecstatic experiences.

Worship can include these elements but worship is far more than these expressions. Worship is a life style, a synonymous for music at our church we have the worship first and the teachings! This is a big misunderstanding because every part of a church service is an act of worship; praying, scriptures, singing, silence, being still, listening to a sermon, taking notes, giving an offering, baptism, communion, signing a commitment card. Even greeting other worshipers actually worship predates music. Adam worshiped in the Garden of Eden, but music is not mentioned until Genesis 4:21 with the birth of Jubal. If worship were just music then all who are nonmusical could never worship. Worship has nothing to do with the style, volume or speed of a song. God loves all kinds of music because he invented it all – fast and slow, loud and soft, old and new. You probably don't like it all but God does! If it is offered to God in Spirit and truth, it is an act of worship. Christians often disagree over the style of music used in worship, passionately defending their preferred style as the most biblical way of honoring God. But there is no biblical style of music notes in the bible, we do not have the instruments they used in Biblical times. Frankly the music style you like best says more about you – and your background and personality – than it does about God. Ethnic groups, music styles, can sound like noise to another but God likes variety and enjoys it all. There is no such thing as "Christian" music, there are only Christian lyrics. It is the words; that make a song sacred, not the tune.

There are no spiritual tunes, if one plays a song for you without the words; you would have no way of knowing if it were a Christian song. Worship is not for your benefit, we worship for God's grace. When we worship, our goal is to bring pleasure to God, not ourselves. If you have ever said, I didn't get anything out of worship today. You worshiped for the wrong reasons; worship is not for one it is for God. Of course most worship services also include elements of fellowship, edification and evangelism and there are benefits to worship but we do not worship to please ourselves. Our motive is to bring pleasure to our creator. In Isaiah 2:9 God complains about worship that is half-hearted and hypocritical. The people were offering God stale prayers, in-sincere praise, empty words and manmade rituals without even thinking about the meaning. God's heart is not touched by traditional worship, but by passion and commitment. The Bible says these people come near to me with their mouth and honoring me with their lips but their hearts are far from me. Their worship of me is made up only of rules thought by men. Worship is not a part of your life; Worship is not just for church services; we are told to worship him continually and to praise him from sunrise to sunset. In the Bible people praised God at work, home, in jail and even in battle. Praise should be the first activity when you open your eyes in the morning and the last activity when you close them at night. David said, I will thank the Lord at all times, my mouth will always praise him, every activity can be transformed into an act of worship when you do it for the praise, glory and pleasure of God. Offering yourself to God is what worship is all about. This act of personal surrender is called many things; consecration, making Jesus your Lord, taking up your cross, dying to self yielding to the spirit. What matters is that you do it. God wants your life – all of it. Ninety five percent is not enough!

There are three barriers that block our total surrender to God; fear, pride and confusion. We do not realize how much God loves us, we want to control our own lives, and we misunderstand the meaning of surrender. One doesn't surrender to God unless you trust him but you cannot trust him until you know him better. Fear keeps us from surrendering, but love casts out all fear. The more you realize how much God loves you, the easier for surrendering becomes. How do you know god loves you? He gives you main evidences; God says, he loves you, you are never out of his sight, and he cares about every detail of one's life. He gave you the capacity to enjoy all kinds of pleasures, he has given us free will to do as we want and he is lovingly patient, forgiving us of our sins. The Lord loves us infinitely more than we can imagine. He gave sacrificed his only begotten son for our sins. Christ died for us and wanted you to know how much he loves us, remember he was crucified for our sins as he was saying I love you this much, I would rather die than live without you! We accept our humanity intellectually, but not emotionally. When faced with our own limitations we react, irrational, anger and resentment. We want to be taller or shorter, smarter, stronger more talented, beautiful and wealthier. We want to have it all and we become upset when it doesn't happen. Then when we notice that God gave others characteristics we do not have, we respond with envy, jealousy and self pity. Surrendering to God is not passive resignation, fatalism or excuse for laziness. It is not accepting the status-quo. It may mean the exact opposite; you know you are surrendered to God when you rely on God to work things out instead of trying to manipulate others, force your agenda and control the situation. You let go and let God work. You do not always have to be in charge, the Bible says, surrender yourself to the Lord and wait patiently for him. Instead of trying harder, you must trust more, and also know you have surrendered when you do not react to criticism and rush to defend yourself. Surrendered hearts show up best in relationships. You don't edge each other out; you do not demand your rights and you are not self serving when you are surrendered to the Lord. The most difficult area to surrender for many people is their money. Many have thoughts as "I want to live for God but!!! I also want to earn enough money to live comfortably and retire someday. Retirement is not the goal of a surrendered life, because it competes with God for the primary attention of our lives. Jesus said, you cannot serve both God and money; and where-ever your treasure is, your heart will be there also. The supreme example of surrender is Jesus. The night before his crucifixion Jesus surrendered himself to God's plan. He prayed, "father everything is possible for you, please take this cup of suffering away from me, yet I want your will, not mine". Jesus did not pray, God, if you are able to take away this pain please do so. He had already affirmed that God can do anything, genuine surrender says, "father, if this problem, pain, sickness or circumstance is needed to fulfill your purpose and glory in my life or in another's, please do not take it away." This level of maturity does not come easy in Jesus case he agonized so much over God's plan that Jesus' sweat, were drops of blood. Surrender is hard work, in our case it is intense warfare against our self – centered – nature. "The blessing of surrender", the Bible is crystal clear about how you benefit when you surrender your life to God. First, you experience peace; stop quarreling, like the battle of Jericho. This is the parade; victory comes through surrender. Surrender does not weaken you with God; if you agree with him you will have peace at last and things will go well for you. Next you experience freedom; offer yourselves to the ways of God and the freedom never quits…(His) commands set you free to live openly in his freedom! Third, you experience God's power in your life, stubborn temptations and overwhelming problems can be defeated by Christ when given to him, as Joshua approached the biggest battle of his life. He encountered God, fell in worship before him and surrendered his plans. That surrender led to a stunning victory at Jericho. This is the parade: Victory comes through surrender. Surrendering to God you do not have to fear or surrender to anything else. Surrendered people are the ones God uses. God chose Mary to be the mother of Jesus not because she was talented, wealthy or beautiful but because she was totally surrendered to him. When the angel explained God's improbable plan, she calmly responded, I am the Lord's servant and I am willing to accept whatever he wants. Nothing is more powerful than a surrendered life in the hands of God. So give yourselves completely to God. The best way to live! Everybody eventually surrenders to something or someone. If not to God you will surrender to the opinions or expectations of others, to money, resentments, fear, ones pride, lust, ego and you were designed to worship God – and if you fail to worship him you will create other things (idols) to give your life to, you are not free from the consequences of that choice. I heard a pastor say; about twenty-five years ago if you do not surrender to Christ you surrender to chaos. Surrender is not the best way to live; it is the only way to live. Nothing else works. All others approaches lead to frustration disappointment and self – destruction. The King James Version calls surrender "your reasonable service" another version translates it to "the most sensible way to serve God". Surrendering your life is not a foolish emotional impulse, but a rational intelligent act. The most responsible and sensible thing you can do with your life as Paul said, "So we make it our goal to please him"; your wisest moment will be those when you say yes to God. Sometimes it takes years, but eventually you discover that the greatest hindrance to God's blessing in your life is yourself! One has stubborn pride and personal ambition! You cannot fulfill God's purposes for your life, while focusing on your own plans. If God is going to work in you, it will begin with this. So give it all to God; you're past regrets, your present problem, your future ambitions, fears, dreams, habits, weaknesses, hurts and hang ups. Put Jesus Christ in the Driver's seat of your life and take your hands off the steering wheel. Do not be afraid; nothing under his control can ever be out of control. Mastered by Christ you can handle anything like Paul; "I am ready for anything and equal to anything through him who infuses inner strength into me, that is I am self sufficient in Christ's sufficiency" (Roman 5:10).

Since we were restored to friendship with God by the death of his son while we were still his enemies, we will certainly be delivered from eternal punishment by his life.

God wants to be your best friend. Your relationship to God has many different aspects; God is your creator, Lord and master, judge, redeemer, father, savior and much more! But the most shocking truth is this; almighty God yearns to be your friend; in Eden we see God's ideal relationship with us: Adam and Eve enjoyed an intimate friendship with God. There were no rituals, ceremonies or religion; just a simple loving relationship between God and the people he created. Un-hindered by guilt or fear, Adam and Eve delighted in God and he delighted in them. We were made to live in God's continual presence but after the fall; that ideal relationship was lost. Only a few people in the Old Testament had the privilege of friendship with God. Moses and Abraham were called "friends of God", David was called "a man after God's own Heart" and Job, Enoch and Noah had intimate friendship with God; but fear of God not friendship was more common in the Old Testament. Then Jesus changed the situation when he paid for our sins on the cross. The veil in the temple that symbolized our separation from God was split from top to bottom. God was once again available, unlike the Priest of the Old Testament who had to spend hours preparing to meet him, we can now approach God anytime. The Bible says' "now we can rejoice in our wonderful new relationship with God. All because of what our Lord Jesus Christ has done for us in making us friends of God". Friendship with God is possible only because of the grace of God and sacrifice of Jesus. That God would want us to become better friends is hard to understand, but the Bible says, "He is a God who is passionate about his relationships with you". Knowing and loving God is our greatest privilege, and being known and loved is God's greatest pleasure. God says, if someone wants to boast, they should boast that they know and understand the Lord… "These are the things that please the Lord. It is difficult to imagine how an intimate friendship is possible between an omnipotent invisible, perfect God and a infinite sinful human being.

It's easier to understand a master-servant relationship, a creator – creation relationship or even Father – Child relation. You will never grow a close relationship with God by just attending church once a week or even having a daily quiet time. Friendship with God is built by sharing your entire life experiences with the almighty. Of course it is important to establish the habit of daily devotional time with God. The Lord wants more than an appointment in your schedule. He wants to be included in every activity, conversation, problem and everything in your thoughts. Practicing the presence of God is a skill a habit you can develop. Just as music practice scales every day in order to play beautiful music with ease, you must think about God at different times in your day; you must train your mind to remember God. Sometimes you will sense God's presence; other times you may not. We do not praise God to feel good but to do well! Your goals are not a feeling, but a continual awareness for the reality that God is always present and worship should be in your life.

One has been meditating continually for the last seven years! We always tell our brothers and sisters at church, that meditation is the best medicine for any illness or condition. The Bible repeatedly urges us to meditate on who God is; what he has done and what he has said! You cannot love God unless you know him, and you cannot know him without knowing his word. The Bible says; "God revealed himself to Samuel through his word". God still uses that method today; Meditation is often misunderstood as some difficult, mysterious ritual practiced by isolated monks and mystics. But meditation is simple focused thinking; a skill anyone can learn and use anywhere. When you think about a problem over and over, in your mind; that's called worrying; when you think about God's word over and over in your mind; that is meditation; if you know how to worry you already know how to meditate. You just need to switch your attention from your problems to Bible verses. The more you meditate on God's word the less you will have to worry about things in general. The reason God considered Job and David his closes friends was that they valued his word above everything else, and they thought about it continually throughout the day.

Job admitted "I have treasured the word of his mother more than my daily bread". David said, "Okay, how I love your law, I meditate on it all day long". They are constantly in my thoughts; I cannot stop thinking about them. The more time you spend reviewing what God has said, the more you will understand the "secrets" of this life that most people miss. The Bible says, "Friendship with God is reserved for those that show reverence to him with them alone he share the secrets of his promises. "Prayers lets you speak to God, Meditation lets God to speak to you" both are essential to becoming a friend of God!

You are as close to God as you choose to be, like any friendship you must work at developing your friendship with God. It won't happen by accident, it takes desire, time and energy. If you want a deeper, more intimate connection with God, you must learn to honestly share your feelings with him. Trust him; when he asks you to do something. Some people are criticized because by their actions, even if you are trying to find some place to meditate without interruption and to finish personal goals in life. One has to thank God because there are brothers and sisters from church understand when God calls on you, you should listen!

This is a temporary assignment and God will allow one to continue with ones duties, then God will take a person back to his surroundings with God's permission. God does not expect one to be perfect, if perfection was a requirement for friendship with God, we would never be able to be his friends. None of God's friends in the Bible were perfect. Fortunately because of God's grace; Jesus is the friend of sinners in the Bible, the friends of God were honest about their feelings, often complaining, accusing and arguing with their creator. God, however did not seem to be bothered by this frankness in fact he encouraged it. God allowed Abraham to question and challenge him over the destruction of the city, Sodom and Gomorra. Abraham pestered God about what it would take to spare the City, negotiating with God, down from fifty righteous people to only ten. God also listened patiently to David's accusations of unfairness betrayal and abandonment. God did not slay Jeremiah when he claimed that God had tricked him. Job was allowed to vent his bitterness during his ordeal and in the end God defended Job for being honest and he rebuked Job's friends for being inauthentic. God told them "you haven't been honest either with me or about me – not the way my friend Job has...... My friend Job will now pray for you and I will accept his prayer".

In one startling example of the friendships God honestly expressed his total disgust with, was Israel's disobedience. He told Moses he would keep his promise to give the Israelites' the Promised Land but Moses would not be able to enter for his disobedience. "God was fed up and he let Moses know exactly how he felt. Moses speaking as a friend of God responded with equal candor; "look, you tell me to lead these people but you do not let me know whom you are going to send with me.... If I am so special to you let me in on your plans... I can't forget these are your people your responsibility....

If your presence doesn't take the lead here, call this trip off right now. How else will I know that you're with me and your people? Are you traveling with us or not? God said to Moses, "all right, just as you say, this also I will do, for I know you well and you are special to me" Can God hand that kind of intense honesty from you? Absolutely! Genuine friendship is built on disclosure. What may appear as audacity

God views as authenticity? Until we mature enough to understand that God uses everything for good in our lives. We harbor resentment toward God over our appearance, background, unanswered prayers, past hurts, and other things we would change if we were God. My wife has a horrible pain on her neck going on two years now! She has been to many doctors and chiropractors she has taken all the medications as directed by doctors.

You may have been passionate with God in the past but you have lost that desire. That was the problem of the Christians in Ephesus – they had left their first love. They did all the right things, but out of duty not love.

If you have been going through motions spiritually, don't be surprised when God allows pain in your life. Pain is the fuel of passion – it energizes us with an intensity to change what we normally posses. "Pain is God's metaphor; it is his way of arousing us from spiritual lethargy. Your problems are not punishment; they are wake-up calls from a loving God. God is not mad at us, but he is mad about our shortcomings and he will do whatever it takes to bringing you back into the fellowship with the Lord. But there is an easier way to reignite your passion for God; start asking God to give it to you, and keep on asking until you have it. Pray throughout your day; dear Jesus more than anything else, I want to get to know you're intimately. God told the captives in Babylon, "when you are serious about finding me and want it more than anything else, I will make sure you won't be disappointed." When Jesus said; "Love God with all your heart and soul" he meant that worship must be genuine and heartfelt. It is not a matter of saying the right words; you must mean what you say. Heartless praise is not praise at all. It is worthless, an insult to God. When we worship, God looks past our words to see the attitude of our hearts. The Bible says "man looks at the outward appearance, but the Lord looks at the Heart". Real worship happens when your spirit responds to God not some musical tone. In fact, so sentimental, respective songs hinder worship because they take the spotlight off God and focus on our feelings. The biggest distraction in worship is yourself – your interest and your worries over what others think about you. Christians often differ on the most appropriate or authentic way to express praise to God, but these arguments usually just reflect personality and background differences. Many forms of praise are mentioned in the bible, among them confessing, singing, shouting, standing- honor, kneeling, dancing making a joyful noise, testifying, playing musical instruments' and raising hands.

You do not bring glory to God by trying to be someone he never intended you to be. The Lord wants you to be yourself. "That is the kind of people the Lord is out looking for; those who are simply and honestly themselves before him in their worship pleases him. When our worship is thoughtful, Jesus commanded to "Love God with all you mind" is repeated four times in the New Testament. God is not pleased with thoughtless singing of hymns, perfunctory praying of clichés, or careless exclamations to "Praise the Lord", because we cannot think of anything to say at that moment. If worship is mindless, it is meaningless you must engage your mind. You have heard people say, "I cannot make it to the meeting tonight, but I will be with you in spirit". Do you know what that means? Nothing is worthless, as long as you are on Earth; your spirit can only be where your body is. If your body is not there, neither are you. In worship we are to offer our bodies as living sacrifices". The Lord wants us to live for him! However, the problem with the loving sacrifice is that it can crawl off the altar and we often do that.

Real worship costs, David knew this and said; "I will not offer to the Lord my God sacrifices that have cost me nothing" but worship costs us our self-centeredness. You cannot exalt God and yourself at the same time. You don't worship to be seen by others or to please yourself. When Jesus said "Love God with all your strength", He pointed out that worship takes effort and energy. It is not always convenient or comfortable, and sometimes worship is a sheer act of the willing sacrifice.

Passive worship is an oxymoron; when you praise God even when you don't feel like it, when you get out of bed to worship when you are tired, or when you help others when you are worn out you are offering a sacrifice of worship to God. "God is real, no matter how you feel". It is easy to worship God when things are going great in your life – when he provides food, friends, family, health and happy situations, but circumstances are not always pleasant. How do you worship God then? What do you do when God seems a million miles away? The deepest level of worship is praising God in spite of pain, thanking God during trial, trusting him when tempted, surrendering while suffering and loving him when he seems distant. Friendships are often tested by separation and silence; you are divided by physical distance or unable to talk. Your friendship with the Lord must have meaning or you would not feel close to him. "Life is all about Love".

The most important lesson he wants you to learn on earth is how to love. It is in loving that we are most like him. So love is the foundation of every command he has given us; the whole law can be summoned up in this one command; "Love others as you would like to be loved". Learning to love unselfishly is not an easy task. It runs counter to our self – centered nature. That's why we are given a life time to learn. Of course God wants us to love everyone, but he is particularly concerned that we learn to love others in his family. The Bible reads; the only thing that counts is faith expressing itself through love and the importance of things can be measured by how much time we are willing to invest in them.

The more time you give to something, the more you reveal its importance and value. God has restored our relationship with him through Christ, and has given us this ministry of restoring relationships; 2nd Corinthians 5:18. As soon as I am finished, writing this book I must practice the lessons in this book in all relationships.

I talked to my wife today Saturday 20, 2010. I told her, God willing I should be finished within two weeks, because life is all about learning how to love; God wants us to value relationships and make the effort to maintain them instead of discarding them. Whenever there is a rift, a hurt or a conflict the Bible tells us that God has given us the ministry of following Christ for this reason a significant amount of the testament is devoted to teaching us how to get along with one another.

Paul wrote; "If you have received anything at all out of following Christ; if his love has made any difference in your life; if being in a community of the spirit means anything to you…. agree with each other, love each other, be deeply spirited friends. Paul thought that our ability to get along with one another is a mark of spiritual maturity, because you were formed to be a part of God's family and the second purpose of your life on earth is to learn how to love and relate to others. Listening is one of the most important skills one can develop. To avoid conflict is by being a better listener; that's why we must pray for the Holy Spirit's continual guidance.

Peacemaking is an art of communicating, always giving and taking, acting like a doormat, and allowing others to always run over you is not what Jesus had in mind. He refused to back down on many issues, standing his ground in the face of evil opposition. As believers of the Lord, we must learn to settle our relationships with each other.

Here are seven (Biblical) steps in restoring fellowship. Pray to the Lord for guidance before talking to the person. If you will pray about the conflict, first, instead of gossiping to a friend, you will often discover that either God changes your heart or he changes the other person without your help. All your relationships would go smoother if you would pray more. As David did with his Psalms, use prayer to ventilate vertically. Tell God your frustrations, cry out to him for he is never surprised or upset by your anger, hurt, insecurity or any other emotions. So tell him exactly how you feel.

Most conflict is rooted without understanding and fellowship. Some of these needs can only be met by God. When you expect a friend, spouse, boss, or family members – to meet a need that only God can fulfill, you are setting yourself up for disappointment and bitterness. No one can meet all your needs except God. The Apostle James noted that many of our conflicts are caused by the lack of prayer. What causes fights and quarrels among us is misunderstanding. Instead of looking to God, we look to others to make us happy and then get angry when they fail us. God says, "Why don't you come to me first". In conflict, time heals nothing it causes hurts to fester. Acting quickly reduces the spiritual damage to you. The Bible says, "sin, including unresolved conflict", "blocks our fellowship with God and keeps our prayers from being answered, besides making us miserable. Job's friend reminded him, "To worry yourself to death with resentment would be a foolish, senseless thing to do, and you are only hurting yourself with your anger".

"Paul advised"!

CHAPTER 12
BEING THE LOVING FAMILY

"Look out for one another's interests, not just for your own". The phrase..."look out for" is the Greek word scoops from which we form our words telescope and microscope. It means pay close attention; focus on their feelings, not the facts of being sympathetic, by listening to understand the context of solutions.

Don't try to talk to people if they are inattentive. Just listen and let them express their emotions without being defensive. Feelings are not always true or logical, in fact, resentment makes us act and think in foolish ways. David admitted, "When my thoughts were bitter and my feelings were hurting, I was as stupid as an animal". We act beastly when we hurt! The Bible reads, "a man's wisdom gives him patience; it is to his glory to over look an offense". Patients come from wisdom, and wisdom comes from maturity and the perspectives of others. People don't care of feelings until they know we care for them. It is a sacrifice to patiently absorb the anger of others, especially if it is unfounded. Remember, this is what Jesus did for you. Enduring tortures in order to save us from our sins; Christ did not indulge his own feelings... As the scripture's say; the insults of those who insult you, fall on me. In the past, I made a lot of mistakes and in my first six months in exile. As I look back on my life and the rearing of my children, I ask myself did I do anything wrong? Well; with time, understanding and living this long life; has taught me that; we learn as we travel through our life's journey. Mistakes come and go, but the lesson of those mistakes should help avoid committing the same.

I have been praying; and understand that there were different ways to be an authoritarian parent, and I understand my shortcomings.

I was unrealistic, insensitive, and very demanding!" The Bible reads; "if we claim we are free of sin, we are only fooling ourselves". So, from now on, I will do my best to do everything possible on my part to live in peace with everyone".

Peace always has a price tag; it often cost our self – centeredness; and sometimes our pride. Jesus said, "You are blessed when you can show people how to cooperate instead of competing and or creating unhealthy discussions". "Ephesians 4:3, reads". You are joined together with peace through the spirit, so make every effort to continue together in this way. Nothing on earth is more valuable to God than his Church; he paid the highest price for it and he wants it protected; especially from the devastating damage that is caused by division, conflict and disharmony.

If you are a part of God's family, it is your responsibility to protect the unity of your fellowship. As believers we share one Lord, one body, one purpose, one father, one spirit, one hope, one faith, one baptism and one love! We share the same salvation, the same life. The same future – factors, far more important than any differences we could enumerate.

We must remember that it was God who chose to give us different personalities, backgrounds, race and preferences, so we should value and enjoy those differences, not merely to tolerate them. God wants unity not uniformity. But for unity sakes we must never let differences divide us.

Only the Lord can decide right or wrong". Whenever I judge another believer, four things instantly happen; I lose fellowship with God, I expose my own pride and insecurity, I set myself up to be judged by God, and I harm the fellowship of the Church. "The Bible calls Satan "the accuser – of our brothers". It is the devil's job to blame, complain, and criticize members of God's family.

Any time we do the same, we are trying to deceive; and doing Satan's work for him. The Bible reads, "Let's agree to use our energy in getting along with each other. Help others with encouraging words; do not drag them down by finding faults." Gossip is passing information when you are neither part of the problem nor part of the solution. People who gossip about other people will also gossip about you. During frustrated moments, because of problems or circumstances, things that come into mind; I ask myself, "Why is this happening to me? Why am

I having such a difficult time?" One answer is that life is supposed to be difficult. It is what enables us to grow. Remember, earth is not heaven! Many Christians misinterpreted Jesus' promise of the abundant life, to mean perfect health, a comfortable lifestyle, constant happiness, full realization of your dreams, an instant relieve from problems through faith and prayers. In a word, they expect the Christian's life to be easy. They expect heaven on earth. This self absorbed perspective treats God as a genie who simply lives to serve you in your selfish pursuit of personal fulfillment. The Lord is not your servant, and if you fall for the idea that life is suppose to be easy, either you will become severely disillusioned or you will live in denial of reality.

Why would God provide heaven on earth when he is planned the real thing for you in eternity? God gives us our time on earth to build and strengthen our character for heaven. The Bible reads, "As the spirit of the Lord works within us, we become more and more like him and reflect his glory even more". This process of changing us to be more like Jesus is called sanctification. You cannot reproduce the character of Jesus on your own strength.

New Year's resolution, will power, and best intentions are not enough. Only the Holy Spirit has the power to make the changes God wants to make in our lives. The Bible reads; "God is working in you giving you the desire to obey him and the power to do what pleases him", but it is still your choice. 2nd Corinthians 4:17 read, "For our light and momentary troubles, are achieving for us an eternal glory that far outweighs them all". Jesus warned us that we would have problems in the world. No one is immune to pain or isolated from suffering, and no one gets to skate through life's problems. Every time you solve one obstacle another is waiting to take its place. Not all of them are big, but all are significant in God's growth process for oneself.

Peter assures us that problems are normal, saying; "Do not be bewildered or surprised when you go through the fiery trials ahead, for this is no strange, unusual thing that is going to happen to you"

March 21, 2010 my grand-daughter, Tracy (My Te-Te) as I call her, was married. Because of my own isolation I missed the wedding and my heart was sad but it was my fault. I know that deep inside of her heart, she wanted me to be there, because of the circumstances of life I was a no-show.

You will never know that God is all you need in this life time, life evolves' around the things that happen including your mistakes, your sins and your feelings. It includes illness debts, disasters, divorces and death of loved ones. Paul said, "We know that these troubles produce patience and patience produces character" Your circumstances are temporary, but your character will last forever. When Habakkuk became depressed because he didn't think God was acting quickly enough, God had this to say; "These things I have plan would not happen right away. Slowly, steadily, surely the time approaches when the vision will be fulfilled. If it seems slow, do not despair, for these things will surely come to pass. Just be patient, they will not be overdue a single day! Blessed are the balanced, they shall outlast everyone".

"The Lord's devastation of the earth" See, the Lord is going to lay waste on the earth and devastate it. "He will ruin its face and scatter its inhabitants – it will be the same for priest, people, masters, servants, mistresses, maids, for sellers as for buyers, for borrower as for lenders, for debtors as for creditors. The floodgates of heaven are opened, the foundation of the earth shakes. The earth is broken up and the earth is split, the earth is thoroughly shaken. In that day the Lord will punish the kings on the earth. They will be herded together; they will be gathered into prisons and punished for many days! Very few will be saved!

"The Lord has spoken"

In closing; all of the people in the original group that worked together back in 1972 are deceased. I am the only one left of the original group. I accepted the Lord Jesus Christ in the year 1955 when I discharged from the Army. In 1956 I was baptized in the First Baptist Church in Waukegan Illinois. I began serving the Lord faithfully. By attending Bible classes singing with the chores in church. I was rewarded by my wife, when she bought me a brand new Baldwin piano for father's day. I took three years of piano lessons, but never excelled to be a pianist in Church. I was more interested in singing, with a tenors' voice. Twelve years after I was Baptized, I turned my back on the Lord, that was 1968 and I will never forget, because that was the biggest mistake I have ever made in my life. My 3 children were 17, 16 and 15. I started drinking with friends, dancing, singing at halls and taverns, having affairs with women. Thank God my wife knew there was some good in me. I always went to work sober and never missed a day of work. We always had a good house but not a good home and that was my fault. I did not understand wisdom, and did not recognize what happened to me as a child, would affect my actions. I could make choices to correct what happened to me. I have written my short comings earlier in this book. I was blinded by evil forces that existed in me. The word of God in the book of Proverbs, Chapter 2; reads, "my son, if you accept my words and store up my commands within you, turning your ear to wisdom and applying your heart to understanding, and you call out for insight and cry aloud for understanding and if you look for it as for silver and search for it as a hidden treasure, then you will understand the fear of the Lord and find the knowledge of God".

For the Lord gives wisdom, and from his mouth came knowledge and understanding. He holds victory for the upright; he is a shield to those who walk blamelessly, for he guards the course of the just and protects the ways of his faithful ones." Then you will understand what is right, just and fair, for every good path for wisdom will enter your heart and knowledge with pleasantness to your soul. Discretion will protect you and understanding will guard you. Wisdom will save you from the way of wicked intentions for men whose words are perverse, who leave the straight paths to walk in darkness. Who delights in doing wrong and rejoice in the perverseness of evil will surely fail at the Lords blessings. I have made many mistakes in my life and continued to make them, but the Lord has blessed me and still receiving blessings. "Amen"

PREFACE

To my Great-Grandson:
Jacob Hanlin
and my Great-Granddaughter:
Giana Hunter
With love and wonder:

To my Nephew:
Frankie, Lucy & Ms. Madanski
For helping with this Book

Special thanks to:
The First Baptist Church in Waukegan, Illinois
for their most heeded prayers.

My Sister in Law Josephine & Julita
I am very grateful to them.
Thank you for your spiritual assistance

It is in Christ that we find out who we are and what
we are living for. Long before we first heard of Christ;
He had his eye on us, had designs on us for glorious
living, part of the overall purpose he is working out in
everything and everyone.

Ephesians I: II

REFERENCES

The Prayer of Jabez Devotional Bruce Wilkinson Author of the #1 New York Times Best Seller The Prayer of Jabez Devotional published by Multmomah Publication, Inc, Post Office Box 1720, Sisters, Oregon 97759, 2001 by Bruce Wilkinson

Love and Anger by Nancy Samalin, First Published 1991, by the Penguin Group Viking Penguin, a division of Penguin Books USA Inc. 375 Hudson Street, New York, New York 10004

The Purpose Driven Life, by Rick Warren, Zondevervan, Grand Rapids, Michigan 49530

Positivity by Barbara Fredrickson, PH. D., Crown Publishing Group, a division of Random House, Inc., New York

Santa Biblia – Holy bible, Bible Text: New International Version, Sociedades Biblicas en America Latina Publicado por Holman Bible Publishers, Nashville, TN 37234

Webster's New World, Compact School and Office Dictionary, Victoria Neufeldt, Editor in Chief, Andrew N. Sparks Project Editor, Macmillan-USA